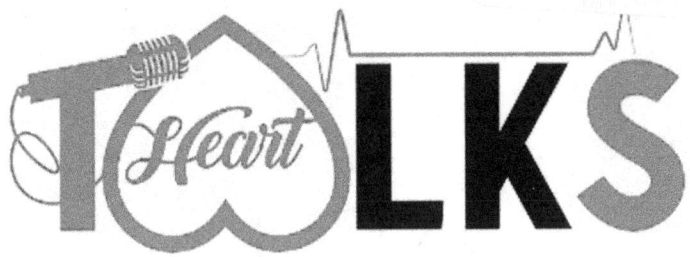

*23 Writers Share Their Journey on
Moving Forward After Struggles*

by

PATTIE GODFREY-SADLER

Volume Editor: Olivia Whiteman

PUBLISHER
New Life Clarity Publishing
United States

New Life Clarity Publishing
205 West 300 South, Brigham City, Utah 84302
Http://newlifeclarity.com/

The Right of Pattie Godfrey Sadler to be identified as the Author of the work has been asserted by her in accordance with the Copyright Act 1988.

New Life Clarity Publishing
name has been established by NLCP.
All Rights Reserved.

No part of this publication may be reproduced, distributed, or transmitted in any form or by any means, including photocopying, recording, or other electronic or mechanical methods without the prior and express written permission of the author or publisher, except in the case of brief quotations embodied in critical reviews and certain other noncommercial uses permitted by copyright law.

Printed in the United States of America
ISBN- 978-1-0880-5160-3
Copyright @2022 Pattie Godfrey~Sadler

Dedication

This book is dedicated to all the beautiful souls seeking to enhance their journey to their heart space in this lifetime.

We are all divinely created for greatness.

Acknowledgements

A sincere message of gratitude to the authors of this book, who believed in me and allowed me to create with them. You have truly shared your hearts and I look forward to hearing more from you in the future. This book would not have been possible without your trust, participation, and willingness to share your voices.

I would like to thank Olivia Whiteman for her endless support and work on editing and cheering me on.

To those who needed any of these messages today. Bless you and I hope you find what you are seeking. May these stories enter your heart and be life changing.

Letter From the Publisher

All the stories in this book are real. Each story is in the writer's voice and spelling from where they live. The essays demonstrate the many ways people seek to move forward in their lives. This book has a common theme of people sharing from their heart how they moved from pain, suffering and disappointment. Whether their struggle was financial, emotional, physical or a combination of difficulties, they found a way through. Some of the varying approaches included prayer, traditional medical treatments, or metaphysical experiences.

Each chapter begins with a passage directly taken from the essay to give you a sense what the writer's story is about. It is my hope that the stories shared will inspire you or make you realize that if you are going through something similar that you are not alone. You will make it through.

Please be open minded about things that seem foreign to you, or that you would never do or do not believe in. We are all unique and believe and experience things differently. I trust there will be value for you in the stories in this book. Remember, we are all divinely created for greatness!

Pattie Godfrey-Sadler
PUBLISHER
New Life Clarity Publishing

Table of Contents

- Creating The Life You Love & Deserve 1
- Live The One Hat Life! 7
- Connecting The Dots 15
- You Are On Stage! 21
- Mom, I Can See Your Light! 27
- TEDX Me Not 33
- Are You Willing to Change the World? 39
- A Big Hole In My Heart 45
- Conversations That Matter 51
- My Rugged Terrain 55
- H.E.A.L.E.D. 61
- Born This Way 69
- I Cry 75
- From Destruction to Enlightenment 85
- My Son's Love 93
- Where Is The Love? 101
- Releasing Fear 109
- From Living And Fearing Death To Living And Loving Life 117
- A Letter to 18-Year-Old Me: A Little Life Advice 125
- Tinker 131
- Lalaland – A Safe Place to Be 141
- The Day I Became a Priority in My Life 149
- Fighting For Forgiveness 155
- Leave A Legacy For Your Family 163

DEE SAVOIE: Dee comes from a powerful lineage of seers, healers, root women and mediums. She has always been both a strong dreamer and an adept interpreter of dreams. Fascinated by the use of symbols and images prevalent in her dream world, she picked up her first deck of Tarot cards at age 14. She has been reading on and off ever since. She currently works with the Goddess Tarot and other decks. As a coach, Dee helps her clients tap into their own intuition and the guidance they receive from their helper spirits to awaken their true Goddess nature. In so doing she inspires them to envision and manifest their grandest dreams for their life, their love, and their work. As an intuitive healer, Dee uses her knowledge of Reiki, mediumship, essential oils, sound healing, Shamanism and dream work to provide individualized healing experiences for her clients. Dee uses chanting, toning, singing, rattling, drumming, crystals, or other modalities, as needed. In all things, Dee facilitates, but Spirit guides. deesavoie.com.

FINDING MY LIFE'S PURPOSE

CREATING
THE LIFE YOU LOVE & DESERVE

> *We can only love anyone as much as we love and care for ourselves.*
>
> *~ Dee Savoie*

A few years back, I was in need of a createthrough. It seemed that everything in my life was falling apart. I had lost my job that I loved, through no fault of my own. My agent, who helped me publish more than a dozen romance novels had died, and my editor left for another job, effectively orphaning my books. My marriage, which had started out strong, was failing. Even a skin condition I'd coped with from childhood had gone wild, covering most of my body. I felt like I had fallen into a deep hole and daylight was so far away that I couldn't see a way out. Something had to give, and I just couldn't seem to get it done on my own. I felt I had one recourse left–I decided to pray!

Each day I lit a candle and said a prayer to the Goddess, and each day I picked a card from my Doreen Virtue Goddess Oracle card deck for inspiration. The first day, I shuffled the deck, spread out the cards face down before me and picked a card–Butterfly Maiden. I really appreciated the sentiment she represented: transformation. Exactly what I needed. The second day, I lit my candle, said my prayer, shuffled the deck again and got–Butterfly Maiden. Every day for 21 days, despite shuffling and cutting the deck, I somehow selected Butterfly Maiden. But, by the end of those 21 days, my skin condition had cleared up. I'd moved out of my apartment with my children, leaving my husband behind. I'd made plans to go back to work in a new and more advantageous position. I recognized I wanted to let my writing career slide for the moment. I also put my healing practice on hold a bit longer in order to cocoon myself for a while. When I returned to my practice, I came back much stronger, with a new direction and a new way of working with women that I knew would be more beneficial for them and myself than I had been doing before.

My name is Dee Savoie and today I am a Life Transformation Coach and Intuitive Healer. I help women discover their authentic selves to live with greater passion, purpose, juiciness, and joy!

I call myself a life transformation coach rather than the usual transformational life coach for one big reason. Transformational coaching is often about making incremental life changes to better serve the client in their everyday life. Life transformation coaching is about making huge shifts in how you see yourself and the life you desire to live. I guess it's because I have been there myself, but most of my clients seem to have reached that low point in their lives where they know that something has got to give. They know that they can't go on living the way they have been because they no longer want what they wanted before. They are ready to give up what they have to seek out what they desire.

In addiction circles, they might call this hitting rock bottom. I call it a createthrough—this is when life hands you an obstacle (or set of obstacles) that you can't get under, over, or around. All you can do is to create a way through. Let me tell you what I mean.

When I thought about becoming a coach, I knew what I wanted to do was bring creative, transformative insight into women's lives. We don't always recognize it, but we are the co-creators of our lives. We are all creative souls. When we accept and embrace our innate ability to influence our own path, we can really bring forth life and newness and change. But I also recognized that for many women, trying to refashion their lives, there's a lot of healing that needs to happen before they can move on.

Most women hold their trauma in their wombs. This trauma can come from birth trauma or ancestral influences, as well as lived experiences. The same thing can happen from a physical wound to this energy, like a hysterectomy, miscarriage, abortion, or other surgery. We need to heal these physical, emotional, or energetic wounds. At first, I didn't realize that this was what I was doing before I returned to my healing practice. I just thought I was "crying it out." It wasn't until I took my first womb healing class that it began to click for me that I had stuffed my pain all the way down into that deep well and I could cry myself a river if I didn't directly address the grief and disillusionment I felt.

I had to go through my own dark night of the soul in which I faced some hard truths about myself and my life and some of the choices that I had made. Once, I had gone through my own healing, I could return to helping others heal.

I developed my signature healing process—Sacred Womb Activation, which assesses, clears, strengthens and reinvigorates womb energies. Most women who have gone through the process have one of two types of results.

1—those who want to become pregnant do (I have a 75% success rate, so far) or

2—any woman not with the right man will find another.

These are actually side effects, though, as most women find themselves opening the business they've always wanted or being able to set boundaries with intrusive family members for the first time, or, most importantly, learning to love themselves in ways they never did before. And that is the true goal of all coaching and healing, isn't it? To help the person we are working with become more completely who they were meant to be. To help them discover their authentic and powerful self and aid them in bringing what they truly desire to fruition for them.

This is what brings joy to me in my practice. More than anything else, I try to focus my life and my practice on self-love and self-care. We can only love anyone as much as we love and care for ourselves. Like a tree that can only grow as high as its roots can support it, we can only love others as deeply as we love and care for ourselves. This is why I would

Hearttalks

like to offer readers a special e-book I created to help women support their own self-care. To download, please go to https://bit.ly/34KIVFR.

I hope my story has helped inspire you to recognize those aspects of your life that may be holding you back because they need healing. Sometimes it is easier to ignore pain or stuff it down like I did, than it is to face it, fix it, and move on. If you would like to find out more ways you can heal and care for yourself, please feel free to contact me at deesavoie.com.

Dee Savoie

GILLIAN STEVENS: Wellbeing has been Gillian's lifelong pursuit, personally and professionally as a high school educator and guidance counselor. Confronted with a mental health crisis, due to an intensely emotional separation, she realized to support her children and students, she needed to prioritize her health. Passionate about helping others, her books provide hope and support for helpers who feel overwhelmed with job demands and the breakneck speed of life. Gillian believes one choice, one action at a time we can create the flourishing life we deserve and transform the world, leading by example. She helps others by sharing her lived experiences and wisdom in presentations and providing guidance to individuals.

Explore, Transform, Flourish: Your SELF Guided Journal to Health, Happiness and Getting What You Want!

2021 Canada Book Award Winner

www.linkedin.com/in/gstevenssg
www.instagram.com/authorgillianstevens
authortgillianstevens.com

FINDING MY LIFE'S PURPOSE

LIVE THE ONE HAT LIFE!

> *We are here, in human form, to experience life and for our soul to evolve and to grow. Just like the spirals in the Nautilus shell, we are perfect as we are, and beautiful and strong.*
>
> *~ Gillian Stevens*

"It's impossible, said pride. It's risky, said experience. It's pointless, said reason. Give it a try, whispered the heart.

Taking the path less travelled to live an extraordinary and authentic life is not for the faint of heart. What you feel in your core, those feelings and fluttering in your gut, are evidence of the very whispers that encourage you to do what seems risky, exciting, and a little impossible. Coeur, the French word for heart, forms the root for the word courage and following our dreams, and doing what feels right in how we live our lives. That choice seems to fly in the face of what we've been taught and witnessed as 'normal', and what's safe and secure leading to success.

He who dies, with the most toys wins! On the surface that's a funny phrase but it implies an underlying seriousness that depicts our belief in success as achievements and acquisitions. We're taught to pursue education and careers that highlight our interests and aptitudes with the promise we'll be met with great success. These acceptable and expected choices are supported and encouraged by our parents, teachers, and society. We strive to achieve success in a "do, have, be" manner focused on surviving at all costs in a dog-eat-dog competitive world. As time marches on we become disconnected from what really lights us up, settling into mediocrity with little time and energy in the joyful pursuit of our passions, should we even be aware what's missing in our lives. In the busyness of life, we become disconnected from our soul and it's only through pausing either through choice or by circumstance aka crisis we re-consider and rise to the challenge of living in our heart. This is my story, breaking apart to falling together and living on purpose.

In high school I was introduced to the sport of competitive swimming and improved quickly intuitively knowing how to move my body efficiently through the water. Determined to improve my times I was dedicated to training, interested in the physiology of swimming faster and stroke mechanics which led to a university degree program in Kinesiology. My swimming success led to a coaching position and as a coach I had to learn how to translate my experience and knowledge in explanations to swimmers to help them improve their times and skills while developing their feel for the water. It was the practical application of my education challenging me to help swimmers reach their goals.

Based on my observations and high school experience I had no interest in becoming a physical education teacher. Ah, the arrogance and judgement of youth! However, my undergrad degree, coaching and my interest in science of movement pointed directly at teaching. It seemed a logical career choice that I would follow in our family's profession based on my interests and ability consistent with teaching. I had confidence and communication skills honed from working with swimmers and as a high school teacher I transferred what I learned as a coach into what would be successful in the classroom. I made a point of recognizing each individual student that passed through my door, aware of the importance of connection and relationship.

I was hired as a supply teacher and striving for the holy grail of a full-time position, representing the security we've all been taught to seek. Unable to obtain a full-time position, I took a leave from teaching and relied on my undergraduate education and interests. I've always looked for opportunities that challenge me and seek knowledge to meet the demands of a job. As a swimmer, coach and physical education teacher, cardiovascular health, and awareness of the physiological demands on the body during exercise and superior athletic performance intrigued me. I took courses focused specifically on the heart's anatomy and physiology, ECG reading interpretation of exercise response and anomalies, and that led to a brief time at a hospital conducting exercise stress tests and administering ECG 's pre-post-surgery, and for admissions. The heart in all its facets has always interested me.

Eventually I had full time employment as a teacher and then later moved into a guidance counselling role, specifically related to student success and supporting students at risk of not graduating due to a number of barriers. If it's important to connect with students as a teacher, it's even more important to be able to connect and build rapport when emotions are at stake. Wanting to meet these students where they were, and as my teacher professional development was lacking training and information related to grief, substance abuse, mental health, and trauma, I pursued workshops that addressed these topics.

Raised in a middle-class family by parents who had immigrated from Britain I had been protected from the family experiences of death, unaware of addiction, and mental health concerns. The path of least resistance was to pursue a teaching position and live a life like everyone else. I had gotten married to another professional, had children, and awaited the feeling of having arrived. Instead, I was unhappy, unhealthy, and felt I had been sold a bill of goods. My "education" however wasn't limited to teaching.

Experiencing the chaotic ups and downs of living with someone who relied on alcohol to manage life, while keeping it a secret, and the emotional and financial stress of the turmoil led to a personal crisis. I learned resiliency, and gained some irreplaceable life skills for success, both personally and professionally through a painful and acrimonious separation and divorce. My marriage breaking apart pointed to my own codependent tendencies and assuming responsibility for my part in the separation. I had a breakdown that I would later admit was the breakthrough that planted me firmly on my spiritual path.

For self-preservation and my sanity, I found Al Anon. The God word didn't resonate. However, higher power worked just fine. I could wrap my head around that term. Eventually this led me to Unity, a spiritual community that was non-denominational, heartwarming and I soaked up the spiritual lessons. It was here I felt at home, like I belonged and that I wasn't alone in my struggles. I began to see life obstacles as opportunities for learning and for strength, leading to my growth and soul evolution. If you focus on the hurt, you continue to suffer. If you focus on the lessons, you continue to grow. It was a big shift from victim mentality to that of a victor. The chaos and recovery I lived led to my heart opening. As I expanded, and grew, my views shifted, and I was no longer a fit for my life. It was a result of being invested in things that weren't in alignment with who I was. I began to question my purpose, the meaning of life, the reason for circumstances and began to see the see beyond appearances of events. I could re-frame and shift what happened to experience the lesson.

What was my purpose here, and how did all these events work together so I could offer service to the world? In my life I'd meandered from one position and job to another and couldn't seem to connect the dots. While I could appreciate the timing and sequence of each circumstance and grateful for the learning, I was unable to see how all of it was my gift of offering to the world. In all my positions I came from a place of the novice and inexperience to growing in confidence as my skills evolved. It was my experience and knowledge, aka wisdom, and trusting my gut, aka intuition, and being present with love and compassion for who was sitting in front of me that helped me. In each role, teacher, parent, coach, friend, I could see my impact, the ripple of vibration outward impacting others. However, I was unable to see the bigger picture and how all of it fit together? This awareness evaded me for a very long time. I was a slow learner and didn't put this learning into practice until much later.

I truly loved my job, helping others, both students and the teachers that supported them. I had dusted myself off, after the self-worth problem accompanying codependency, and gained some ground. I regained my self-confidence. As I approached the last five years of my career I encountered a shift in my administration, which resulted in a significant change in my work life and my emotional state and enjoyment of my job. It affected my health and wellbeing. The stress contributed to weight gain, as my exhausted adrenals interplayed with my hormones, and I couldn't seem to release the weight. I lacked the energy to do any exercise and even walking my dog became a chore. I decided to retire. Leaving my job led me to conclude there was more to life than feeling tired, stuck, and unhappy. It took courage to leave my job early, hitting my pension, yet my self-worth and wellbeing were worth it.

I trusted my intuition and put myself first. I followed my heart. When my colleagues asked me what I was going to do when I left teaching, without skipping a beat, I answered, I was going to write a book. I had very bravely at times pondered writing. However, I had no clue how, no plan, not even a solid idea to write about so this honest answer took me a bit by surprise.

I did write a book and in fact I have completed three now. My books emphasize the necessity for us all to prioritize our wellbeing, as we are all helpers. I realized that as a single parent if I was not healthy, and put myself first, I could not be there for both my children and my students in the way they would need me. Based on my experience as a counsellor and the lack of necessary education regarding trauma, grief, addiction and mental health, my books also highlight the need for helpers to have the most relevant and up to date information and strategies, so they have the confidence and comfort level to be of prime assistance with their children, students, clients, and patients.

Writing and sharing my life in print has been the scariest, most challenging, and yet rewarding projects. Scary because you put yourself out there. There is no hiding. Once you put something in print, it's there forever and readers gain insight into who you are. It took me almost a year to write my first book, to be unafraid to share my ideas, and overcome the self-doubt as a novice author. When I did the final edits before publication, I had to once again confront the doubt as I had changed, naturally, from the initial writing to editing phase.

The second book was easier, and it felt almost like cheating as it relied on the first book, and was much less writing, as it was a companion journal.

My most recent book, was intended to be an update of the first book and I naively thought it would be completed quickly, however it took on a life of its own as now five years after the release of the first book, a lot has changed, within me, and the contents of the book. The book addresses burnout, empathic strain, vicarious resiliency, and highlights the idea the community or collective care, acceptance in the workplace, and of the need to prioritize personal wellbeing is essential. I have found my purpose and joy in sharing what I have experienced and learned and delight in helping others.

"All journeys outward ultimately lead to the journey inward, where everything you seek already exists and awaits your joyous acceptance" Alan Cohen

I have evolved as a writer, as a human, and spiritually through my life experiences. The consistent themes in my life have been that of emerging, nudging, resistance and eventual acceptance and pursuit of that adventure. I love the simple yet stunning beauty of the Nautilus shell. I even have some jewelry that reminds me of this shell. It is a metaphor for the spiral of growth and a symbol of beauty, strength, and perfection. Its beautiful smooth shell suggests elegance and perfection with brown and reddish stripes. Within it are sections that are depressed and compressed, and the shells are so strong they can withstand pressure at depths of 2600 feet beneath the surface of the ocean. The spiral and sections in the shell suggests that the creatures it houses will grow forever. Similarly, we never stop growing, learning, and expanding. This is a powerful metaphor for our spiritual evolution.

I finally got it! We are here, in human form, to experience life and for our soul to evolve and to grow. Just like the spirals in the Nautilus shell, we are perfect as we are, and beautiful and strong. We need our bodies to be strong and healthy, as vehicles for our souls so that we may experience life. We are here to remember we came from love, and our mission is to love ourselves through it all. As we love ourselves the love spills out, and onto others through our passion for what we do, as we follow our heart's lead. In reflection, every job, every opportunity was a chance for me to express love, beginning with what was comfortable and easy, swimming, to coaching, to teaching and as my confidence grew, my

Live The One Hat Life!

challenges expanded to include my life lessons and eventual recognition of my purpose. My falling apart was really everything falling into place!

Wayne Dyer said, 'what someone thinks of me is none of my business' and that has become a guiding principle for my life. As a parent, and as a person, I have made choices in alignment with my beliefs and values even when it's uncomfortable. It is simply who I am. However now with the acquired wisdom and confidence that comes with age, I'm even more steadfast in my beliefs and choices, and even less concerned what people think of me.

It has been said, how you do one thing is how you do everything, and Dr. David Hawkins urges us to live a one hat life. This is a simple phrase reminding us to be consistent in our behavior, in alignment with our values in every and all situations, personal and professional. That is being truly authentic! Who we are is simple. We are love! When we show up, expressing our passion for life and sharing our unique gifts with the world, we encourage others to do the same.

Listen to the whisperings of your heart. The perfection, beauty and strength of the Nautilus shell is who you are: strong, perfect, and beautiful. Keep learning, growing and ever evolving as the spiral within the shell. Be courageous and live your most authentic life. You'll find it is rich with possibilities and opportunities.

Gillian Stevens

HEIDI SCHALK: Heidi is a Mindset and Business Strategy Coach who helps entrepreneurs scale their businesses to multi-six figures and seven figures online. She is a native Floridian, born and raised in South Florida and mom of two children and three dogs. She is also active advocate for animal rescue. Heidi began her entrepreneurial journey due to finding herself at the divorce table and now empowers women with the tools and strategies to confidently build successful, online businesses, using their skills and talents. She helps them claim the life of their dreams so they can care for the people and organizations that matter most to them and to create the life they desire, on their terms, so they can have the freedom to enjoy life with their family and loved ones. You can find her on social media and through her website https://heidischalk.com

FB: https://www.facebook.com/heidi.lupischalk
IG: @heidischalkcoaching Website: https://heidischalk.com

> FINDING MY LIFE'S PURPOSE

CONNECTING THE DOTS

> *Anyone can have an incredible life they love if they follow their heart. It just looks different for each person. It's about getting clarity and the willingness to be unapologetic about what you want.*
>
> *- Heidi Schalk*

I had a journey that was very scary. If asked if I had to go back and do it all over again, would I? The answer would be in an instant YES! Why? Because I learned so many lessons along the way. Lessons I needed to learn to be where I am now. I learned how to trust and surrender. I learned how to create intimate and connected relationships and being an introvert, I definitely learned about communication and how to overcome my fear of being seen and heard.

All my life I struggled to make ends meet. It wasn't an easy road. It always seemed like there were so many more days left in the month than money. And my relationships... well let's just say, that didn't come without its challenges as well. I got married days before my 35th birthday and I became a stay-at-home mom a year and a half later. We continued to struggle on and off for a few years until things got better with work for my husband. Unfortunately, two kids and five animals (three dogs and two cats) later, the marriage ended in divorce. I was now a stay-at-home mom who needed to figure things out...and quickly. Not being an income earner for ten years I wondered, "how was I going to generate an income to take care of me, my kids, and animals? I was scared, yet I trusted.

I trusted I would find the way. For the next two years after my divorce, I worked two jobs. I had big goals and aspirations and knew working a 9-5 wasn't going to get me what I wanted to achieve and so I also started a business. It was a roller coaster of wondering if I was ever going to make it. I was run down and burning out. Not everyone was onboard with my business goals. My family didn't understand my "coaching" business and asked me why I wouldn't just look for a long-term job where I could collect a steady paycheck for the next 25 years or go back to school?

During this time, I found Les Brown, a motivational speaker and Lisa Nichols, from *The Secret on YouTube*. They were my inspiration to go after my dreams. I continuously listened to them. It was when I heard Les Brown say during one of his speeches, "The graveyard is the richest place on earth, because it is here that you will find all the hopes and dreams that were never fulfilled," that I fully committed to doing whatever it took to stay on the road of being an entrepreneur and never give up. I had to remind myself everyday where I wanted to be and how bad I wanted it. Every day I thought about being on my deathbed and looking back over my life and what it was going to look like. Was I going to look back and have regrets for not going after my dreams or was I going to look back with joy and no regrets? I chose no regrets. I put my stake in the ground and kept going as I knew that I wanted to be home with my kids.

I was willing to do whatever it took to reach that goal. I found mentors to guide me with the skills I needed. In fact, one of my mentors shared a quote from Steve Jobs that literally changed the trajectory of my life and business. It was then that things really shifted for me in a big way. The quote is: "You can't connect the dots looking forward; you can only connect them looking backwards. So, you have to trust that the dots will somehow connect in your future." I've grown so much since I started my journey. I'm not the same person I was. I'm a stronger version of me. I'm a more intimate version of me. I am a more connected and more vulnerable version of me. I am willing to take risks and step

Connecting The Dots

through the fear and know that no matter what happens, I've got this, and that is far from where I was when I first started just a few years ago. It took me awhile to understand, but I now know the beautiful thing is anyone can have this.

Anyone can have an incredible life they love if they follow their heart. It just looks different for each person. It's about getting clarity and the willingness to be unapologetic about what you want.

This is your life. Not your parent's or anyone else's life. Clarity is about really knowing your vision for your life, and how your business and other people fit into it. It is about letting go of trauma, learning from your "learning lessons," and knowing that each step is a dot that will connect in your future and trusting in those dots. Trusting in yourself. When I finally listened to my heart unapologetically, the dots started to appear, and doors started opening.

Fast forward to today, I am no longer burning the candle at both ends. I am home with my kids and dogs every day. My schedule is directed by me, not someone else or a 9-5 job. Vacation time is whenever I choose it to be. I love my life and I am living it on my terms. I now live my life every day based on that quote by Steve Jobs. I've learned how to see my "mistakes" or "failures" as learning lessons and the next step forward to where I am going. I've learned to love the journey and the "mis-steps." I am always growing and evolving. We all are and if there is only one takeaway you received from my story, I hope it is to not settle.

Too many women settle, and I had done it my entire life. I did what other people thought I should do and what they thought was right for me. My family didn't understand what I was doing and why I started my business, but today they are all proud of me. It may not have been what they would have chosen for me, but I love my life. Often, when I wake up in the morning and make my coffee, the house is quiet. The kids are upstairs sleeping. Two of my dogs are sleeping in their bed and the other is on the couch waiting for me to sit with him as I write my morning gratitude. I usually look outside over the lake as the sun is glistening over the water and say to myself how much I love my life.

I feel so blessed to be where I am at this moment. I am happy. I'm grateful for every single step that has brought me here because without each step… without each "mistake" … each "failure" … I wouldn't be here in this moment right now. My journey continues and I couldn't be more excited for it. Years ago, my focus was on my business for myself and my children, and I am so grateful for every step along the way. Now I get to choose me. I get to open my journey up to finding my person. To find the person I get to share my life with and create our life together. And I trust every day that the Universe, God, is working in my favor and in my best interest. I move through each day of my life one dot at a time, trusting and knowing that they will connect in the future, and enjoying each step along the way.

My hope for my story is to inspire you to get to the next place in your life. No matter what it is. Get clear on your vision for you, not for anyone else and do not give up. I want to gift you the quotes that motivated me. May they inspire you to choose you and never give up as they did for me. Visit me at https://heidischalk.com/gift.

Heidi Schalk

MICHAEL VAN BUTSEL: Michael is a Certified Transformation Coach with Success Journey Academy. He lives in Bradenton, Florida on a small ranch with rescued animals including horses and donkeys.

> HONORING OUR PARENTS

YOU ARE ON STAGE!

> *Many times, we do not realize the dramatic impact our daily routines have on those who surround us, watch us, and delight in us.*
>
> *- Michael Van Butsel*

The management icon, Jim C. Collins has written remarkable corporate strategy books that can also apply to your personal life. His works include one book titled, *Good to Great*. His management advise includes a story of choice, discipline, and predictability which achieves remarkable results in the corporate world, and if used in your personal life, it can also have significant impact. This impact can occur as we take "stage" in every phase of our lives. Many times, we do not realize the dramatic impact our daily routines have on those who surround us, watch us, and delight in us. Our role is important to them. For example, many members of the boomer generation are taking care of their aging parents as they enter the senior years. It is challenging and demanding role. It is a journey. We have shared the journey with my mother aged eighty-eight, who passed in 2009 and now, again with my father-in -law who is still an active 85-year-old. We would like to share where our journey took us with my mother and the surprising results of predictability and a final moment where divine resonance intervened to calm the heart and tears of a six-year-old little girl, her granddaughter, Alexis.

We flew my mother and grandma to Florida from Nebraska and entered her into an assisted living facility (ALF) on the west side of Bradenton, Florida. It looked just like the typical single-story sprawling building hidden on the side street tucked behind a Ronald McDonalds fast-food drive through. Every Sunday and several Wednesday afternoons, we were "on stage." My daughter Alexis, age six and I would visit my mother. We became a regular show with everyone. We passed the front desk and greeted the nurses and the social worker. Sometimes, we saw the operator of the beauty shop and thanked her for grandma's weekly hair appointment. My mother lived on the west side of the large central social room, and we would pass in front of the gallery of seniors who passed the day watching the Fox News channel and the guests who came to visit. There were usually about 40-50 people. They smiled and giggled and waved to Alexis. They all wanted to know what we had brought for her grandmother this time. It usually included a cup of coffee from McDonalds and a hash brown. Sometimes, it included a flower and a little chocolate. We had a routine which was important to grandma, the staff at the ALF, the other residents and to us. Grandma's eyesight was progressively getting worse, but she would use her index finger to find the little hole on top of the coffee cup from McDonald's. Alexis would tell grandma about our dogs, cats, horses, and donkeys on our little ranch and grandma sometimes would surprise her with a tea set or stuffed toy.

After about two hours, we would wrap up our visit and make the trek back to the entrance, across the gallery of the social room and front desk. We were on stage and did not realize, at the time, how our visits were important to so many. It seemed like a normal day to us that just repeated over and over again. It was life of caring for an elderly mother. But we were on stage! But being on stage was so much more important than we realized. We became actors for the residents of the ALF and the staff. We did not realize the weekly visit of a son and granddaughter was not the usual norm. The fact we came every week at the same time became important to my mother, her fellow seniors, the ALF staff and even the staff at the McDonald's. The fact our schedule was so disciplined and predictable, people looked forward to seeing us.

For those seniors who did not have the same family support, we became a delight to them and elevated my mother as someone who was important to her family. They lived by extension to our visits. So, the visits lasted for about 18 months until my mother became severely ill and started to cycle in and out of the hospital. Until finally, we challenged the doctor to recommend hospice. I had to meet everyone at the hospital. I came into the hospital and greeted the hospice manager who had me sign all the documents to transfer my mother to hospice care. When the final form was signed, the hospice manager walked over to the nursing station and declared "Mrs. VB is now transferred to the hospice protocols." A wave of relief came over the nursing station and they immediately started to get my mother comfortable for her relocation. The hospital nursing staff saw what we as the family had also realized.

It was the last time I saw my mother conscious, but she had also agreed to the decision. It really did not hit me about the decision to move my mother to hospice until I arrived at my mother's room in the hospice center. The hospice nurse came into the room and posted a big red DNR flyer on the bulletin board near the entrance of the room. It read "DO NOT RESUSCITATE" and below it showed my signature. I asked myself.... what had I done? At the time, I was working on a large project four hours away. The following week, the hospice director called and said the time was nearing for my mother to pass away. I left immediately, but my mother still unconscious, passed away before I returned. However, my mother's last moments were not alone. My wife, Susan, Alexis and my older stepdaughter, Krysta were there. My mother had been unconscious since they moved her from the hospital. But the girls had stopped by the hospice to just be there. The girls had also picked up a snack.... you guessed it.... from McDonald's. They stopped in to just let grandma, even subconsciously, know they were there. A few minutes after they arrived, the nurse came out and said grandma had passed away.

After her passing, I asked my friends why me? I had older brothers. One of my more matter-of-fact friends simply pointed out that my mother had trusted me to have the courage to "sign the DNR" ....do not resuscitate. He said she did not know if the older sons would have the courage to step up and make the tough decision. Then, my friend with his usual candor and humor said, because you were the baby and the favorite. So, we needed to go back to the nursing home to collect my mother's belongings.

As we started through the painful process of sorting through her belongings, many of her friends and acquaintances at the ALF stopped by to share their regards and how much they enjoyed my mother and how much she would be missed. But they also said, they would miss Alexis and our weekly visits. We were predictable and had become important to their lives, too. The staff members were also sad with her passing and said they would miss our weekly visits because it showed how important my mother was to our family and how much we respected her.

We had become singular by exception with our visits and had elevated my mother's regard with her friends and the staff at the home. Sad, but true, not every resident at the ALF had family members who came to see them. Our last trip to the ALF ended up taking longer than usual, but when we finished, it was dark outside. My daughter, Alexis, was in the back seat of the car in her safety seat. It was dark in the Jeep. Alexis was quiet for a long while and then quietly demanded, Dad, I want my grandma back!" What do you say? So predictably, I said, "I know sweetheart, but she has gone to heaven." Alexis started to cry and then suddenly, I realized she had stopped. I asked if she was OK and she said in her soft voice, "yes, Dad I am ok. God told me grandma was with him and he is going to take care of her now. He promised he would do a good job. I am ok." I was pleasantly stunned. His grace descended upon our family. We had been on HIS stage of life, too, with his divine guidance. Our simple weekly routine had become an important and rewarding memory for many people surrounding my mother in her last few years. It had become a treasure to our family without realizing it.

We honored my mother with a memorial service back in Nebraska. About seventy-five people came to the service. It was held at the Assisted Living Facility where she had lived several years before moving to Florida. It was a quiet and sober service, but two comical events did occur at the service. A woman, who I could not remember got up and gave

You Are On Stage!

a glowing recall of my mother. I was sitting by my oldest brother and whispered, "who is she?" He did not know. After the service, even after she came over to greet us, I asked the funeral home director who she was. He said, "well, she shows up at a lot of the memorial services (it is in the newspaper/obituaries) and tells everyone how great their loved one was. I guess you could call her a funeral groupie. She does not do any harm and warms up the show for the members of the family."

My mother also had a good sense of humor and had directed me to share the recipe for her "chocolate chip cookies." They were a big hit in the small town of 1,100 people at all the community events. Everyone knew it was her tradition. However, she had refused to share her recipe even with close friends. I announced her decision to share the recipe at the memorial service and there was a gasp among all the ladies...." please share!" I paused and said it was there all the time, printed on the side of the Quaker Oats container.

My brother said later, that was a big surprise. I said, "yes, but Mom also said the real secret was freezing the cookie dough for 3 weeks! She said I could not tell them that." So, what can be routine and predictable may seem unimportant.... however, it is a choice.... a choice and discipline that will produce remarkable results and some benefits that you will not realize at the time. It can impact everyone who has seen you "on stage." I guess you could say it gives you a chance to go from GOOD to GREAT!

Michael Van Butsel

JULIANN CUNNINGHAM: Juliann has spent over 40 years studying, practicing, and helping others heal through yoga, Tibetan meditation, Reiki, Macrobiotics (whole food energetics of cooking). Juliann has spent years teaching yoga and lecturing in New York, Tennessee, Texas, and Northern California. Juliann has brought yoga to many, healing them from such illnesses as breast cancer, diabetes, fibromyalgia, depression, stress, hip and knee injuries to spinal injuries as well as teaching students to become registered teachers under the National Yoga Alliance. Coordinator, Lecturer, Teacher of healthy lifestyles to individuals, yoga studios, Mount Madonna Yoga Center affiliate Santa Cruz, Ca, corporations, hospitals, health clubs and continues to lecture and teach nationally to annual conferences, Nashville Yoga Society, National MS Association, Fibromyalgia Support Groups, Kindermusik Organization, FONI of Nashville as well as dance studios, churches, hospitals, and schools. Juliann is a member of Nashville Yoga Society, CTYA of California and National Yoga Alliance. Juliann Baker Cunningham, RYT 500/E-RYT 500 National Yoga Alliance certified to teach students teacher training, brings over 40 years of experience in studying and teaching yoga following in the tradition of Krishnamacharya teachings on the healing benefits of yoga. Juliann has studied Alexander Technique (correct body alignment) with Master teachers Daniel Barach and Chris Stevens. Juliann has also studied under an array of other great yoga masters such as Tim Miller, Ashtanga yoga teacher training, David Life and Sharon Gannon, Jivamutki Yoga, Richard Freeman, and Erich Schiffmann. The foundation of her studies and teachings honor the great master, Sri T. Krishnamacharya. Juliann sees things not as they are but as they can be. By understanding that we as humans are so much more than physical. Healing comes on a spiritual level so the body can heal the physical body. Juliann feels that with mindful practice and discipline we can bring balance and harmony physically, mentally, and spiritually for a better sense of overall wellbeing.

> HONORING OUR PARENTS

MOM, I CAN SEE YOUR LIGHT!

> *You know you are on the right track when you become comfortable in your own stillness.*
>
> *~ Juliann Cunningham*

My dad once told me, "Babe, life is but a dream." His words sank deep in my heart throughout my life. I am left constantly contemplating on their meaning. Throughout our lives, each of us play several different roles. Some of mine are daughter, wife, mother, grandmother, teacher, healer, and friend. As I reflect on my life, I realize that I have an endless number of stories to tell. In this essay, I have chosen to talk about the one closest to my heart. This is a story about my mother and her final days on earth. A time which came totally unexpected. Humbly, I had the privilege to assist on my mother's journey in crossing over.

My mother's name is Dorothy. She was born in 1930 and lived to be just two months' shy of her 88th birthday. Mom was an amazing woman. Although we didn't always see eye to eye on many things in life, we always felt close in our hearts. My mother was a woman who put her life in God's hands and spent her time in service to many, many people. A beautiful role-model, I find that I am much like her in so many ways. As a daughter, I watched my mother give so much of herself to her family. It seemed like every day Mom would be tending to the needs of others as well. Our home was a house that welcomed everybody, surrounded with faith, hard work, play, laughter, and love.

Throughout the years, Mom gave unconditional love and service to anyone in need. At the end of her life, there could never be enough deserved recognition for all she did. It started in May 2018 when I took my daughter and her two young sons to visit my Mom at her Senior Living apartment in Upstate New York. At the time the boys were around one and two years old. Mom had not yet met the youngest grandson. It is a 17 ½ hour car trip from Tennessee to Upstate New York to visit grandma. We stayed at my mom's for five days, taking her for rides back to her old homestead in Jerden Falls where she was born and raised. She loved it! Jerden Falls is all woods now with reminiscence of foundations left among the trees. We used to ride up to Jerden Falls as kids, mom and dad would tell us stories of home life there. Mom was very happy to be with us. It was a special, memorable time I will always cherish.

When it came time for us to leave, we gave our loves and said our goodbyes. As I was walking to the car something told me to go back in the house one more time to hug my mom and tell her once again that I loved her and how much she meant to me. Somewhere in my consciousness I must have known it would be the last time I would see my mom as she always was.

Even though we lived far apart for all those years I always felt close to my mom. Although we were not able to be together in the physical realm, we were always spiritually connected in a very special way. Less than a few weeks after we arrived home in Tennessee, I got a call from my brother. "Mom had fallen and hit her head." It took several hours before anyone found her. Apparently, there was a light outside over her door in which if something happened to her, she could turn it on and someone would come. This time, she couldn't get to her light. Strangely enough, the light came on, without her activating it. Thank God it did, because someone saw it and came running to her room to find her. To me, this was a miracle. The doctors found that Mom had fractured her head and a section of bone was loose. The surgeon told us that he could stabilize the bone structure. Mom came out of the operation with flying colors! We were all relieved. It looked like Mom was going to be okay! Then, several

Mom, I Can See Your Light!

nights after the operation, the doctors said mom's heart had stopped for several moments then restarted in her sleep. Sadly, the next day we learned that she was brain dead and wouldn't be able to talk to any of us.

I had no say in her medical situations, but two of my older siblings did. After listening to the doctors, they decided to put my mom in hospice. It seemed surreal. I had just been with her having such a good time. All of this happened so suddenly. My husband and I took the 17 ½ hour trip back to Upper New York State. We stayed by her side for the next nine or so days, during which time mom would sometimes open her eyes and talk to me.

At one point she said, "Juli, I don't want to die." It was then I knew, I had to talk her through her journey to the light. Up until then, I had spent my entire adult life learning healing techniques. Both of my parents were proud of me and honored my work. One day, while my mother was in the care of hospice, I took out my pendulum and checked Mom's chakras. I performed Reiki on Mom to help her relax so she could process what was happening in her body. Although Mom and Dad both believed in the Reiki healing process, most other family members didn't know what it was. They thought I was strange.

On the morning of June 12, 2018, I woke exhausted and spoke to Mom in spirit. I said, "Please Mom, let go, we are all so exhausted. Leave your tired body behind and go be with dad in heaven." Shortly after that, we got a call from my brother that mom had passed. When I heard the news, my heart dropped to the floor. My husband and I rushed to be by her side. Her flesh still warm to the touch I prayed for her, told her I loved her. "It's ok to go, Mom. Go to the bright light." All together it had been a more than ten-day journey going to be with Mom and being able to be by her side. After the funeral services, my husband and I drove back to Tennessee. For several nights after we were back, I would feel and see this dark, dark energy hovering over my bed. I told my husband about it. "I think my mother's soul is trapped in the darkness." I was not sure that my spiritual strength and protection was enough to help her because I was exhausted physically, mentally, and emotionally. Going in to pull her out of the darkness would be pretty intense and the need for protection was a must. But the darkness was getting worse. I felt as if I was standing on the outside of this dark energy, looking in, and could feel the dark beings all around her. I had to make the decision to save my mother. I reached my hand into the darkness and told Mom to grab my hand. She seemed so lost, weak, and disorientated as if she didn't know what was happening to her. Finally, I reached down far enough to grab her arm and pull her straight through. I sent her to the light, letting her know she was safe.

After that incident, the darkness never came back. I could feel my mom was in a bright, beautiful, loving place. A few years later someone told me that in that moment, my mother had crossed over in the rainbow body. We are so much more than our physical being. Our thoughts, beliefs, and values are the outer, human substance. The inner substance is our loving heart and spiritual connection to God and Self.

My Tibetan teachers say, "No one person's suffering is greater than another. All suffering is suffering." As we see each other more than physical, we realize the need to help the spiritual. We can grow spiritually by learning the tools we need to help ourselves and to help others. Everyone has that ability to help heal themselves and others, by awakening to our inner divine Self that we came onto this earth with. Those that feel they don't believe or that they don't have that ability I say to you, "Awaken!"

It is truly un-natural to feel the separation from ourselves and God, thinking that we are many different parts, and each part working independently from our authentic self. This can cause us to be in a state of confusion and chaos. In our monkey minds we tend to think we are all this, all that, or nothing at all. Where is our higher self? Where is that understanding of who we really are?

Life begins to make more sense when we learn to recognize our own soul and why we came here. We are light spiritual beings residing in this human body. You know you are on the right track when you become comfortable in your own stillness. Just like many, there was a time when I was confused and lost, contemplating the question, "What is my purpose here in this life?" I had no idea that I am a divine being having the human experience. Years of conflict and self-doubt lead me into studying different ways to understand my spirituality. Through yoga and meditation, I discovered my authentic self.

Mom, I Can See Your Light!

The universe leads the way to find the resources. I finally learned how to get out of my own way and just allow myself to be in God's divine light, everything then began to make sense. God's will will be done when your intention is pure and for the benefit of others.

Isvara Pranidhana, pronounced 'Ish-va-ra-pra-nid-hah-na' means to lay all our actions at the feet of God according to Patanjali's Yoga Sutras (2:45). When I learned this, I surrendered my life to God's will and plan. In so doing I became a caretaker for all sentient beings. By replacing my will with God's will, I learned to follow my heart in my efforts to help others.

We are human in our thoughts, emotions, and beliefs. It is on that glorious day of enlightenment that we can learn that we are so much more inside. When we finally completely trust God and learn to listen to that silent, loving voice, this is how we get in touch with our spiritual selves.

Unfortunately, many people stay stuck in 'chitta vritti narodah.' This is the fluctuations of our ego thinking we are all this, all that, or nothing at all. The unknowing of your divine self is the true source of suffering.

Everything in life is interconnected. We are more than flesh and bone. We are more than our thoughts or emotions. We are energy, light, and vibration and with proper intention we connect with our Spirit and transform into our higher Self of oneness. Once we realize this, we understand that the physical is just one small aspect housing us on our journey to the Divine light.

Dedicated to my mother, Namaste, (the light in me honors the light in you).

Mom, I can see your light.

Juliann Cunningham

KELLY KAELIN: Kelly believes that our hearts hold all the wisdom we need; we just need to heed them more often. Listening to the world and not her heart, led Kelly into the world of corporate finance and accounting, through the worlds of film and project management, and finally into metaphysics and spirituality. Reverend Kelly Kaelin is a podcast host, an international best-selling author, a Certified Conscious Transformational Coach, and the Director of Programs for Success Journey Academy. To speed the journey into your own heart, join Kelly on her podcast: The Metaphysics of Life. KellyKaelin.info

HONORING OUR PARENTS

TEDX ME NOT

> *Sometimes, you just have to take action.*
>
> *~ Kelly Kaelin*

When the opportunity of a lifetime comes along, jump on it! It's really a great opportunity and I take it. I jumped in and decided to do a TEDx talk. The coach is top-notch and he's affordable. This guy is amazing. He's run TEDx events for years and knows what matters. The energy of what he is building is palpable. I want to be on THIS journey with THIS coach at THIS time. It's a guaranteed TEDx stage in December 2021. It's a best-selling book in early 2022. It's a plan to build my audience, my credibility, and my visibility all in one year. I'm becoming more visible; I've already started with a podcast. This seems like it's the right time to take this journey and I dedicate myself to it. And my body starts telling me "NO!" . . . in no uncertain terms.

Every time I think about my script, the stage, the traveling, my stomach gets in a knot and my solar plexus tightens up. Anxiety ensues. I want to be on this journey with this coach . . . right now. I want it badly. I want it so, so much. Ugh! Being highly intuitive, I know I must heed what my body is telling me. With a conflicted mind, I withdraw from the program. I tell myself that saying "no" now doesn't mean I won't ever do a TEDx talk. It's just not now and I'm quite dashed and disappointed.

As soon as I withdraw, my body relaxes. I really have no idea why I can't do a TEDx talk right now and yet, somehow, my body knows now is not the time. As the days go by, I forget about my intensely desired journey, focusing on other aspects of my world – work, taking care of myself, my family and friends, my critters, my home, and garden. Pretty standard stuff.

A month or so later, I start getting a nudge to go see my Dad in Texas. So I ask him – "Can I come see you?" He says, "Not yet." Weird answer but I know he hasn't been feeling his best. So, I wait. I don't really want to go. I don't want to fly all day. A few weeks later, I get another, stronger nudge. Dad's answer is the same. It's late October and Dad goes into the hospital for 12 days. He gets stable and goes home. I ask again. "Can I come see you?" And again, he says: "Not yet." Sigh. I still don't want to go and yet, my anxiety is building.

The trip is coming. I can feel it. A brief reprieve in my anxiety occurs when two friends need a place to stay. It's nice to have company in the house and I enjoy it. The critters – two dogs and a cat named Richard - couldn't be happier. The "nudge" is no longer a nudge – it's grown into a push and it's very uncomfortable.

Sometimes, you just have to take action. I'm unsure of why but I know I must go. I tell my friends I need to fly to Texas and see my Dad. They graciously tell me to go. They'll take care of the house and the critters. I talk with my business partners and they tell me that they have my back. "GO!"

It's the week before Thanksgiving and this time, I don't ask. "Dad, I'm coming. Tomorrow." Surprisingly, Dad and my sister, who has been living with him and caring for him during these turbulent times, are both ecstatic. Somewhere between "Hello" and "I'm coming tomorrow," the energy changes. The conversation becomes animated and excited. I get on the plane. I tell myself, my house mates and my business partners, "I'll be back before Thanksgiving."

When I arrive, Dad's eyes are bright and sparkly – like they always are – but he doesn't get up to greet me. He's attached to an oxygen tube. My sister looks exhausted. Apparently, she's been waking up every twenty minutes to make sure Dad hasn't removed the oxygen cannula from under his nose. I'm here to support and I volunteer to stay up with him that night. It's funny . . . she fights with me on this a bit. Then she goes to bed. I stay up with Dad. He doesn't want to sleep, so we talk. We talk about all sorts of stuff – things I know about him and things I don't; things he knows about me and things he doesn't. We talk deep into the night and he starts to doze off. So do I. I wake up and his cannula is off. He doesn't really seem to be sleeping. I swear he's reciting something over and over again. It's odd. Like he is trying to stay awake. I don't understand why this is going on. It doesn't make sense.

Why is Dad not sleeping? My sister said this started when they changed one of his medications – he has congestive heart failure and the doctor changed his diuretic. The other one was working but it was also possibly damaging his liver so they changed it. And he hasn't slept since - even after the diuretic was changed back to the original one. Something's not right. The doctor offered some new sleeping pills. They didn't work. We try some herbs, some Kratom. They didn't work. We try visualization. We are desperate to get him some sleep. He sleeps - well maybe - 20-30 minutes at a time. It's frustrating. I stay up most nights with Dad. Hopefully, this will give my sister enough of a reprieve so that she can continue to take care of him after I go back home.

My sister is doing a great job caring for Dad. It wasn't planned. This all came about because of the lockdowns. She was visiting Dad when the lockdowns started and decided to stay to support him. He is 85 after all. After a year and a half, she is still here keeping him company and now caring for him as he recovers from his most recent hospital stay. I'm grateful. One of the most beautiful moments of my life unfolds as I watch my sister take care of my Dad. She's so fully present, so loving, so genuine in her connection with him. It doesn't take her long – perhaps two minutes – to figure out what he needs in that moment. She then addresses both what he needs and what he wants, as she gives him the gift of her presence the entire time. I smile knowing that her being here with Dad is Divine.

The Divine definitely had its hand in this. Dad still isn't sleeping and I'm feeling the effects of sleep deprivation. I try to stay present remembering I'm only here for a week. I can deal with little sleep for one week.

My sister has been dealing with it for over a month. She needs the break. I doze off, then Dad wakes me by bellowing my name. He wants me to record him and to go through a bunch of boxes to try and find something. I'm not even clear what we're looking for. I'm angry with him for waking me to do such a chore – can't it wait for the morning? Hrumph! I go through probably 20 boxes – still not completely certain of what I'm looking for. As morning dawns, Dad wants to sit in a chair instead of on the couch. We set a chair next to the couch. We pull him up and turn him to put him in the chair. He's heavier somehow and he falls into a slump. He looks glazed and doesn't answer. 911. We think he's had a stroke. The guy on the other end of the phone coaches us. "Dad, say 'The early bird catches the worm.'" Dad says, "The early bird catches the worm and then the worm gives the early bird the finger." Typical Dad! He did not have a stroke and he tells everyone that. The paramedics arrive and Dad argues. He does not want to go to the hospital. The ambulance crew and paramedics pack up and start heading out. The ambulance leaves. Two big paramedics help pull Dad up from the chair and put him on the couch. Dad slumps again. There is no way that my sister and I can support Dad with this new development. Something is clearly wrong. The ambulance is called back. 26 hours later, Dad is gone.

The next week is a blur. I make it back home. My heart is on the floor. Bare. Open. Vulnerable. I'm glad no one is around to step on it. My friends have moved on. More weeks pass. My mind is a whirlwind of thoughts, grief, regrets. My eyes stay red, swollen, and bloodshot.

Three months later, my stomach is still in a knot. I am not over it. Not sure I ever will be. God, I miss my Dad so much! I wish I hadn't been so angry with him when he woke me. I pray he knows how much I love him. The ashes of his body sit in an urn on my favorite corner shelf, waiting to be released into the air from some flying contraption. Dad loved planes and flew his whole professional career. Dad lived a great life and got to do exactly what he wanted to – he flew fighter jets and commercial airlines. I identified planes as "Daddy" before I ever knew what they really were. In one of our late-night talks, Dad said he didn't want to be reincarnated because he couldn't do it better than he did it this time around. If he does come back, he wants to be a vulture

TEDX Me Not

because of the way they fly; playing in the winds of storms and eddies. That's my Dad.

I'm so grateful for my Dad. Grateful for how long he was with me. Grateful for having the chance to see him again before he passed. Grateful for being with him when he passed so he wasn't alone. So, so grateful for the last, deep conversations we shared.

Dad passed a week and a half before I would have been on stage for that TEDx talk. I could have had that TEDx talk under my belt. I could be well on my way to building more credibility, more visibility. I could have been a best-selling author by now. And it all would have been so hollow. I'm so grateful that I had the wisdom to hear and listen to my heart.

Now I understand why my body was so adamant, so insistent that I not take the TEDx stage. My focus and energy was there for my Dad; and I will always treasure our last moments together.

I love you, Dad. God speed. We'll go flying again soon.

Kelly Kaelin

JACKIE SIMMONS: Author and International Speaker, Jackie Simmons, believes in tackling complex and challenging topics and making sense out of them. As the creator of Conscious Transformational Coaching, Jackie believes you deserve to guarantee results for your clients, every session, every time. When you work with Jackie, she's going to offer you some different thought processes. Jackie always shares alternatives to get you unstuck, find out what's true and what's not true – spot the elephant in the room – so that you can have what you want and what you deserve. Jackie and her three daughters are on a mission to make teen suicide a thing of the past. The mission has grown to include two books, three programs, and "The Talk" that saves lives which Jackie presented at TEDx TenayaPaseo in Las Vegas. Jackie believes that you have a right to happiness and a life free from worry. Jackie imagines a world where all emotions are under your control and what other people say and do, says a lot about them, and nothing about you.

BREAKING THE SILENCE OF SUICIDE

ARE YOU WILLING TO CHANGE THE WORLD?

> *If you are willing to risk being judged by the world, the world will bring you the people and the resources that you need to change the world.*
>
> ~ Jackie Simmons

I wasn't. I wasn't willing. I wasn't ready. I wasn't the right person for the job. The good news for me is that my daughter Stephanie was. Thanks to her, on August 3, 2019, my life gained purpose and changed forever.

I've gotten ahead of myself. A good story should have a great beginning, a transformative middle, and a compelling conclusion. This isn't a good story. This is a great story. It's January 2021. I'm speaking to a near empty room in Las Vegas on the one topic that I'm an undeniable expert in and that I wish I wasn't. It's the launch of a brand new TEDx stage. TEDx TenayaPaseo, an ambitious endeavor born out of my mentor Iman Aghay's Inspiring Speakers' program.

In the fall of 2019, TEDx organizer Sarah Jefferson had everything lined up: the venue, the sponsors, the speakers. At the beginning of 2020, with the event scheduled for May, my script and I were both a hot mess. My TEDx coach was an amazing volunteer who called me out for being tactical and not vulnerable. In February I re-wrote my script. I turned away from telling everyone what I thought was wrong with the current system and how to fix it and turned towards what silence is costing us as individuals, families, and communities. My coach Jeff Blanton loved it. I knew that it was a good enough talk, and I've always believed that good enough was just that, good enough. And then in a blink of an eye in March of 2020, courtesy of COVID, it all went away. First the date, then the venue, then the sponsors, and eventually even my coach.

Nature abhors a vacuum. On April 1, 2020, my daughters and I launched a non-profit to take on the "silence" and try to break it. We reached out to schools and school administrators just as the educational system imploded trying to cope with the COVID shutdown. The book that we published sat in boxes in my spare bedroom . . . We started teaching what we thought was the solution, only to discover that while the stress of COVID was making the problem worse, it was also preventing anyone from seeking a solution.

In the midst of COVID, I forgot my own training as a stress management consultant. I forgot that under stress the brain seeks to survive, not solve. We shifted our expectations from in-person trainings to online summits. I interviewed hundreds of experts; unexpectedly, my perspective on the problem started changing. By the fall of 2020, there were rumblings of a new date for the TEDx event.

Then the call came. What?! In eight short weeks I would be flying to Las Vegas! I hadn't flown anywhere in more than a year and a half. I was excited. I pulled my script out of the drawer and started rehearsing. After four weeks of reading, and rereading, and reading out loud, I was worried. All of a sudden good enough didn't seem good enough anymore. I needed a second opinion. At the end of one of our mastermind meetings I asked my friend, and former TEDx organizer, Roger Killen: "Hey Roger, would you read my TEDx script and share your thoughts with me?" "Of course." His Irish lilt making me smile as it always does. We arranged to chat the next day. "Jackie, your content is really good. And I'm afraid that it's not going to inspire anyone." My heart sank at the truth of his words. Honestly my script didn't inspire me either . . . "Would you help me make it better?" "Jackie, you know they don't like script changes within four weeks of the event, and you've only got three. I will only help if you get Sarah's permission."

Are You Willing to Change the World?

To her credit, Sarah said "Yes, you can make changes, IF you'll be able to deliver the new talk with authenticity." My talk topic wasn't changing. In fact, the only reason I was taking a TEDx stage at all was because of the story I had lived. I knew that authenticity wasn't going to be a problem. I had underestimated Roger. "Jackie, to go from vulnerable to inspiring means that you're going to have to stop trying to vulnerably talk about it and get completely naked. Not about your story, Jackie; the story of that day. You're going to have to tell your daughter's story." "Roger, there's nothing more to the story of that day. I was there. There was nothing unusual or special. It was just an ordinary day until there was nothing ordinary about my life. Honestly Roger, I don't remember any more than that." "Can you ask your daughter?"

Hours later with shaking hands I finally dialed my daughter's number. Much to my disappointment, she answered the phone. "Hi honey, no nothing's wrong just a quick question. You know I'm rewriting my TEDx script and honey they want me to tell the story of that day . . ." "I'm not surprised mom." "I guess I'm not surprised either and I'm really sorry. But Stephanie, I don't remember . . ." The silence roared in my ears and the air stopped moving in my body as I waited. The air all came out in a whoosh as Stephanie laughed. I wasn't sure how to respond so I just listened as her laughter rolled on. When she caught her breath, Stephanie said: "Mom, it was the shopping . . ." And then I remembered.

It was June 1995. Stephanie and her sisters were getting ready for their summer visit with their dad and his family one state away. Getting three girls ready for a trip means only one thing, shopping! I had put the memory of that day and many of the days that followed into a brown box stored it somewhere in the deep recesses of my mind. And there it stayed for 23 years. The memory might have stayed buried in the back of my mind forever if it hadn't been for August 3, 2019. On that day, Stephanie (now 37) stood in the front of a conference room audience and delivered the longest seven-minute talk I've ever heard. Her talk had all the right elements: A startling fact: "3,000 teenagers will attempt to take their own lives today in the USA." A personal story: "when I was 14 . . . "A bit of humor: "mom and I had the other talks, the one about sex, the one about drugs, the one about alcohol and then I went to college on a dry campus. That means the kegs are hidden in the showers of the girls' dorm." A shocking revelation: "I still struggle with suicidal thoughts." A brave declaration of intent: "Now I want to teach the coping skills I've learned to teens, before they need them." A standing ovation: audience members rushed up and hugged her and thanked her for being so brave. And in the back of the room, I was frozen; stunned; immobile. Shocked to the core by the struggles that Stephanie had faced alone because I hadn't had the courage to break the silence. I hadn't wanted to know what could cause my daughter so much mental and emotional pain that she would think dying was better than living. Even if I thought for a moment that maybe I could bear knowing, I was too afraid to bring it up. I was afraid of putting the idea back in her head.

After that day Stephanie and I decided to work together. Along with her sisters, we co-founded the nonprofit Teen Suicide Prevention Society. Stephanie's desire to share coping skills with teens before they need them launched a mission to "make teen suicide a thing of the past." The mission got attention and swept her sisters and me along with it. I did my best to duck. I was so grateful that COVID closed Vegas and my TEDx talk had been postponed . . . Nothing prepared me for this talk. Not my 30 years of stress management training, my many years in counseling, my multiple trainings as a speaker. The idea of doing what I had been raised not to do filled me with dread. I had a school administrator for a mom, an Army sergeant for a dad, and a preacher for a grandfather. I learned at an early age that we do NOT . . . . . . air our dirty laundry in public. There's not much dirtier than suicide. In my world, everything touches everything. Because I was going to be on her TEDx stage, Sarah arranged for me to be interviewed on Bruce Barnes' podcast. I returned the favor and interviewed Bruce on The Suicide Prevention Show, the summit we started during the shutdown. Being the host of the summit was no big deal. Being the host, getting other people to share their stories, felt safe. During Bruce's interview I learned that Bruce does amazing things helping people turn around their automatic negative thinking. Bruce introduced me to the transformative tech that he uses with his clients and then to its creator, Kim Serafini. Once I understood that the technology works like a vision-board-on-steroids, I started using

Are You Willing to Change the World?

it every day to prep me for the TEDx ordeal I was heading into. Every day, I got a little more comfortable with the thought that just maybe I was going to be OK. Just maybe I could tell the story and not fall to pieces, or breakdown and cry, or run and hide (missing my flight did cross my mind). By the time I stood on the stage of TEDx TenayaPaseo, I was not only comfortable with myself as the teller of a story my mind had tried to hide from me. Kim Serafini's company came out in support of the mission by helping us create the phenomenal gift of "Emotional Teflon". What I've learned on this journey is that if you're willing to risk being judged by the world, the world will bring you the people and the resources that you need to change the world.

We haven't solved the problem yet. Teen suicide is still a thing. We'd like your help to make it a thing of the past. Please consider watching my TEDx talk on how to have the talk that stops teen suicide. We've been blessed and now what started as a TEDx talk is available on both YouTube and TED.com. More importantly though, please consider changing the world. Show one person that you care, share one extra smile with a stranger, reach out for a hug, take on one limiting belief about what's possible and BUST it. AND above all, please stay. Heaven doesn't need another angel. Heaven knows we need you here.

Jackie Simmons

KELLI HANSEN: Kelli Melissa Hansen Founder of BCC Evolution, is a Warrior for Mental Health and has dedicated her life to save as many lives as possible by normalizing the conversation around mental health and suicide. After losing her middle sister to a completed suicide in 2017, she founded BCC Evolution, a mental health and suicide awareness nonprofit which is on a mission to ACE; increase Awareness, cultivate Conversation, and provide Education.

Kelli has a bachelor's in Communication, minor in Psychology, has an NLP Master Practitioner certification from Worldwide Institutes of Neuro Linguistic Programming, is certified as an Adult and Youth instructor for Mental Health First Aid and is an author in the multiple collaborative books.

She has been featured on Authority Magazine, Thrive Global, The Happy Head Podcast, U.K., Life Story Curator and many more.

www.bccevolution.org
Facebook.com/bccevolution, Instagram.com/bccevolution
https://www.youtube.com/c/BCCEvolution

BREAKING THE SILENCE OF SUICIDE

A BIG HOLE IN MY HEART

> *If we open our minds, hearts, and mouths, together we can make mental health matter.*
>
> *~ Kelli Melissa Hansen*

When you lose a family member to suicide, there are no words. No words that will change the fact, no words that give you reassurance, no words that are ever going to make you feel better. You will never "get over it" and you will never fully understand. Because when someone makes the choice to take their own life, you as a survivor to the loss of suicide are left with a big hole in your heart and so many unanswered questions. However, there is a light at the end of the tunnel and as I have been told many times, you will eventually learn how to grow forward with their beautiful memory. The grief, the disbelief, the pain, the emotions will come and go in waves like the ocean and one day you learn how to celebrate and forgive. Forgive yourself and forgive them. Celebrate their life and celebrate that you are still alive.

I want to take you on a journey, a journey through tragedy and trauma. A journey that turned into love, light, lots of hope and a cause that is bigger than myself. I lost my middle sister Carrie to a completed suicide on February 20, 2017. I remember that day vividly like it happened yesterday. I was sitting at my desk at work and got a call from my mom. It was the middle of the day, and my mom does not normally call as she knows I am at work. I had to let it go to voicemail because I was on a call at the time, but with voicemail to text the message came through and I knew it was urgent. I finished my call and went to the bathroom to listen to the message of my mom crying and telling me something very bad has happened to Carrie and to call her back.

I immediately called her. She was still crying and said Carrie killed herself.

My immediate thought was "wait, what did you say? Are you serious?" My mom replied "yes, we are on our way back from the cabin to go to Carrie's house." My heart sunk, and I felt numb. I didn't know how to react at first and didn't immediately cry because I became very aware of my surroundings, as I was in the women's bathroom at my work.

I hung up the phone, paused for a moment, thought about what my mom had just said, and started crying. I remember a woman coming into the bathroom and asking if I was okay. I am not sure what my response was, but she mentioned that we had phone rooms that were private if I needed it. The first thought that popped in my head was I didn't even know we had phone rooms. But I put myself back together and made my way out to the floor. I assumed that I would be okay to work the rest of the day, but my supervisor could tell something was wrong. So, I had to tell her, and I told her I was leaving for the day.

The thought going through my head was that I had to make it to my sister's apartment before my mom did because she did not need to deal with that. I needed to be strong and take care of things for my mom.

My little sister called me as I was on my way to Carrie's house and told me her husband was on the way to Carrie's and I shouldn't go. I remember feeling so angry and thinking, who are you to tell me what to do? I need to take care of this for my mom and I'm already on the way.

I arrived at Carrie's apartment, there were police and my other sister's husband was outside and Carrie's boyfriend was being questioned by the police. I wanted to go inside so bad to see if it was real. I still was in a haze of it not being real. My nephew, Carrie's son and my mom showed up and hours passed. The coroner showed up and wheeled her body out

A Big Hole In My Heart

of the house. It was real, I couldn't believe she actually did it. I was so mad, so sad, and in shock. I know we all were.

Something you need to understand about my sister Carrie was that she was the one person that I grew up with the most. She was the sister out of five girls that I was the closest to. My life followed similar paths and she was my go-to person for everything. Cooking, cleaning, advice, she was my birth coach for both of my kids, she was the person I looked up to for everything. She helped me file for divorce from a narcissistic drug abuser and always had the perfect answer for whatever question I had. She was a caregiver for a paraplegic, a CPR instructor and had a million friends who loved her dearly. She was a kind, generous, helpful, incredible soul, but in the same breath she drove me bonkers. I called her my "crazy" and "overdramatic" sister. I thought she always wanted attention and I couldn't be around her for really long periods of time. In reality I just didn't understand her.

She had attempted suicide six other times throughout the years, but every other time we all knew when it was going to happen because she would call someone, and we knew to call 911. She spent time in a mental health facility at one point and had several 72 hour holds. I never understood why my sister didn't want to be on this planet. But then she had a botched hysterectomy that almost took her life and for once it seemed like she finally wanted to be alive. She was later diagnosed with Multiple Sclerosis which caused her to be in pain often.

As life does sometimes, I was punched in the face by reality and my sister was gone. Why? I will never know, but what happened instead of sitting around and doing nothing I made a choice that I wanted to start a nonprofit in her honor and gain a much knowledge as possible, so that another family wouldn't ever have to go through what our family did. I wanted to give more understanding to anyone that will listen, so that people that are struggling don't feel so alone like my sister did, and I can save lives. The nonprofit I started is called BCC Evolution, BCC: Because Carrie Cared and Evolution: because we are always evolving. We are a mental health and suicide awareness 501c3 nonprofit. I have found through all the knowledge that I have gained that most of the time the root cause of suicide is due to a mental health challenge whether it is for a moment or a lifetime. That is why BCC Evolution's focus in on mental health and suicide prevention education. I didn't understand what my sister was going through, so I have made it my life's mission to educate the masses and open the conversation about mental health and suicide, so that we break down the stigma and start saving lives.

I will never get my sister back. I will also never fully understand why she left us, why she left her kids and why the choice of taking her life was what she thought was the best solution to a temporary problem. But what I do know is that being a survivor of a loss to a suicide is a rollercoaster and journey that no one understands until it has touched their life. It is not a journey that I wish on anyone or any family. However, if it happens to you or your family, I want you to know there is hope, light and love at the end of the tunnel and you can learn to grow forward and be the light for those that might be struggling too.

Dedicated to Carrie Lyn Parsons 1973-2017

Kelli Melissa Hansen

TAMMY ATCHLEY: Tammy is a Certified Conscious Transformational Coach who focuses on parenting and is an expert in transforming the bullying experience. What do you do when you find out your child is being bullied? Tammy helps you have the conversations that matter with your child. Conversations that keep the lines of communication open and allow you to listen without judgment. Being bullied herself and having a child who was bullied, Tammy is on a mission to end bullying. Tammy teaches "Bully Defense Mastery: How to Bully Proof Your Child" so that you feel confident that you can help your child live through bullying and come out the other side happy, healthy, and safe. Tammy imagines a world where everyone is kind to one another, where bullying is no longer an issue, and no one needs to take her course ever again. Tammy believes in making the world a better place . . . isn't that what we all want for our kids? To learn more about her mission visit: www.TammyAtchley.com

BREAKING THE SILENCE OF SUICIDE

CONVERSATIONS THAT MATTER

> *When someone you love is struggling and you are not sure what to do . . . just be there for them. Let them know you care and then listen. No judgment, no fixing, just listen.*
>
> *- Tammy Atchley*

Have you ever noticed someone you care about start acting differently? They withdraw or seem sad? I'm visiting my friend who just had her first baby. She steps out of the living room while I play with the baby. This precious new baby girl is so beautiful. After a while, my friend comes back into the living room. I can tell something is wrong. She seems sad and I can't imagine why. As we sit on the couch and talk, she shares that her husband is having a hard time. He is sad and depressed. She said that he had had depression in the past off and on but nothing like he is going through now.

As we talk, I realize that my friend isn't sad as much as she is worried. The longer we talk the more she opens up to me. Her husband told her that he didn't want to be here anymore. She's scared sick. "Do you want me to try to talk to him?" "Yes, please."

I walk down their never-ending hallway praying. I pray harder than I have ever prayed in my life. I don't know what to say to him or how I should say it. I knock softly on the wooden door. I barely hear him say "Come in." I open the door slowly and he's lying on the floor in the dark. "Is it okay if I come in?" "Yes, if you want to." I turn on the small lamp, his eyes are bloodshot red from crying and he looks away. "How are you?" "Not so good." "What's going on?" "I'm not sure, I feel worse than I have ever felt in my life." "Did something happen?" "No, I just don't want to be here anymore. I'm sad and I don't know why." He starts to softly sob. Tears flood my own eyes. A couple of years earlier I learned questions to ask if someone was thinking about ending their life. But my mind was totally blank. I start to pray. All of a sudden one of the questions pops into my mind. I ask, "Do you have reasons to stay?" He looks at me troubled and hurt. "Yes," he whispers. His voice shaking. "Tell me one reason you have to stay." "Well, my family of course." I nudge, "Tell me another reason." "My wife, and my baby." I nudged more, "Tell me another reason you have to stay." "My mom, dad, brothers, and sister." "Tell me more reasons you have to stay." He cries even harder, realizing that he has many reasons to stay. The more we talk, the more reasons he gives me. I can tell by his voice that his mood is clearing and the weight on his shoulders is getting lighter and lighter. The sadness is starting to go away. He starts to smile and then to laugh. We start talking about other things as we walk down the hall together. I see the look of relief on my friend's face as we step into the living room together, smiling. I'm amazed that one very simple question brought such a big change.

Before I leave, he's on the phone making an appointment to get help. Asking a question seems like such a small thing but when it changes someone's life, or in the case of my friend's husband, saves someone's life, it doesn't seem so small.

Several years earlier, my seven-year-old daughter came home from school in tears. She looked up at me and said, "I can't take it anymore, mom." She seemed so small and so young to have said those words. "What's going on at school?" She looks down and begins to cry. Not just a few tears but a bucket full. She sobs for what seems like hours, my heart breaking with each passing minute.

When she calms down enough to speak, she says: "Mom this girl at school is so mean, she teases me every day. She tells me I look like a boy because my hair is black, curly, and short and hers is long, blond, and

Conversations That Matter

beautiful. She pushes me and then tells the teacher she didn't do it. Stuff like that happens all the time. She makes me cry and sometimes I can't stop." I hold her hands and look deeply into her big, beautiful brown eyes and tell her how beautiful she is.

We talk for over an hour. We laugh, we cry, we snuggle. Then, in a flash of inspiration, she starts talking about what she could do if someone is mean to her again. "Wow, those are great ideas, I wish you had been around to help me when I was being bullied." I start noticing changes in my daughter. She seems more confident. She isn't crying as often.

Things still happen at school from time to time and she is so proud to tell me how she reacted or didn't react. Sometimes things don't work, sometimes they do. The point is that we talk. We both learn from these conversations. That first talk makes all the difference.

When someone you love is struggling and you are not sure what to do . . . just be there for them. Ask them a question. Let them know you care and then listen. No judgment, no fixing, just listen. Ask your child what they know about bullying. Do they know anyone who's been bullied? These are the conversations that matter. They can make all the difference in the world to those you love and care about.

Tammy Atchley

RITU CHOPRA: Ritu, a technologist by profession, is an author, TV show host, award winning film producer, a certified leadership coach, motivational speaker who is on a deep spiritual journey. With 20+ years of experience in Fortune 500 companies serving in IT operations, information security in global financial, health care industries, she wants to share her knowledge and give back to community. She is Founder and President of Leadership Consulting Services LLC, providing consulting services for leadership development for emerging corporate personnel in IT and Non-IT space for leadership roles. Ritu is also the Founder of Lead My Way, a Not-for-Profit Organization, and is an advocate for Domestic Violence Awareness and Prevention efforts. She is an award-winning documentarian producer and director.

> FINDING STRENGTH, FINDING A PATH

MY RUGGED TERRAIN

> *Life has never come with instructions; we learn and write our own manuals as they fit into our own agenda and outlook on the environment around us. From the dark valleys into the clouds of inspiration, something of higher value was waiting to come out into existence.*
>
> *~ Ritu Chopra*

Where has the time gone? I look around and see my life in fragments scattered everywhere. Dusty layers of time had faded some memories and some that I chose to let go of. I'm reminiscing about how the journey has changed me and I'm listening to its rhythms from my heart.

Now, as I look back, I noticed that sometimes I followed the paths opened to me and other times, I paved my paths. Along these paths are the stories of my life that have been deeply etched. Those paths opened themselves to unite me to the stories to be written on the jagged cobblestones.

I grew up in a loving, protected middle-class home, where the highest education possible was our parents' goal for their children. Then life changed drastically. My higher education was interrupted. As a young, aspiring woman in incredibly challenging circumstances, I had to find strength and meaning inside. A diary my loving dad give me when I was thirteen years old, I filled with the 'golden pearls of wisdom' copied from folk stories, books, newspapers, and anywhere I found them.

After many years of an unhealthy and toxic relationship, facing threats for myself and my family, cultural stigma, shame, fear, uncertainties, and loss of dreams that I began with, my journey was very rough. I was fortunate to have had the education and burning desire to change my life's conditions. I was able to stop the physical abuse that often injured my spirit and my sincerity towards my loved ones.

I questioned myself but protected everyone else from the 'shame and stigma' that comes with breaking away. I was preparing myself to embrace the roughest path and break the cycle of ongoing emotional and verbal abuse. Now and then I found myself picking up the fallen pieces scattered around in the shadows of life, spirits bruised, and confidence lost.

Nowhere to turn to for help, where would you go? Those who are supposed to protect you are those ready to harm you. How can someone reconcile this?

I was trying to find my place in my little universe. How did these challenges fit into the 'ambitious world' that I had imagined growing up?

I was seeking answers and was relying upon the strong values that were embedded in me, and sometimes I felt moving on, spellbound as I was in a crazy 'scene' of a drama of life. I didn't find the answers I was looking for, only more disappointments. It was not easy to let go of the glorious ambitions and fall prey to the vicious claws of destiny. Everywhere I turned, disappointments, hurt, sadness, and then an auto accident left me physically and emotionally in pain.

I remember reading "When life hits you hard and knocks you down, roll over and look at the stars" and these words of wisdom were just the medicine I needed. The faint voices of hope infused with faith emerged into the dark valleys and lifted my spirits. Bright rays of hope as the headlights on the winding roads broke into the darkness, enough for me to see a small patch of the lighted path ahead. So, I looked up and had no choice except to create something out of this misery. Ask and you shall receive, my self-inspired moments gave me the courage to write a book. Oh! 'Into the memory lane again to relive the moment of the past,' I thought to myself.

My Rugged Terrain

My inner voice whispered 'No, go on'.

Seeking answers, I remembered another pearl of wisdom written in my childhood diary-- 'A teacher shall appear when the student is ready.' Wow, life amazes me, several teachers appeared from various walks of life at the right time to guide me through what I needed to understand, and to answer the questions I had in those moments. I crossed paths with many teachers. It seemed like a coincidence to meet strangers once and get answers to my questions, and never to see them again. I was mesmerized by absorbing it all and felt like floating in a cloud of inspiration.

A woman's journey alone continues into the unknown terrain. Life has never come with instructions; we learn and write our own manuals as they fit into our own agenda and outlook on the environment around us. From the dark valleys into the clouds of inspiration, something of higher value was waiting to come out into existence.

I wanted to inspire others, give hope and encouragement, and find the strength to get up and get moving when it hits hard. I had not realized that I was writing another chapter of my journey, a chapter of hope and faith. It gave power to the fainted voices of hope and allowed them to echo into the dark valleys.

Now, it's not just the hope you see, but also an element of faith that rides along with it. Faith has joined hope and the hope that sustains the power in faith. It's like magic, in a sunlit field with fragrant fresh air. I saw this as my calling. I reassured myself it is my calling, not a passing idea. Something bigger was waiting here that I had not imagined before. It drifted my attention from darkness to a destination of a new goal, much more profound to heal the painful moments. It was not time for sadness. I had to do something to take me to a higher plateau. I would often seek guidance from the golden pearls written in the diary Dad gave me.

Writing my first book 'Art of Life' allowed me to dig deep inside and discover a new outlook on the world we face, inner strength, courage, and learn that true happiness is possible no matter the outer conditions presented to us.

Aha! you say, I have learned hard lessons and managed to swim across and stay afloat. Finally, a smooth ride gathering all my strength. I was ready to aim higher.

"Not so fast dear," life whispered to me "You are special. I have another test for you."

The economic meltdown of 2007-08, "The Great Recession" arrives in our lives, snatching away financial security from me instantly, leaving me to grapple with a new reality to deal with. Many uncertainties around, it is not the time to give up now.

Wait, I am too tired, I need some resting moments.

But time does not hold still, and it does not slow down for anyone. Rustling to keep pace with the flow, I was looking for answers, and as a true companion the powerful inner voice whispered again, 'You've been given many chances to grow despite the challenges. You've mastered these skills; you can't stop now.'

I would search my diary for golden pearls of wisdom to find something to ride upon. My second book 'Mastering Life, Exploring Your Untapped Potential to Reach New Heights' became even more of a vehicle for me to ascend from mundane to a higher purpose, giving me a wider range of opportunities to meet teachers who crossed paths with me and gave me rationale and reason to pursue my curiosity.

I assembled the broken shattered pieces one more time, I inventoried my skills and reignited my dreams and aspiration to beat all odds this time. Taking a giant leap of faith, I mean a high jump from where I was to go to a new playing field. Drenched with enthusiasm, courage, and audacity, I had the strategy, product, right market, the right audience, entrepreneurial skills, tools, and technology. All I needed to make it work. Yes, I can make it work I reassured myself.

"Not so fast, you brave ignorant," said Life, "it's a man's world, a woman alone trying to compete in a world of 'privileged' members of our societies. Can you prove your worth to compete with them?"

What I set out to accomplish away from my comfort zone with the hopes to create an opportunity for myself, was yet another stumbling block. Well, yes it was a huge stumbling block indeed. Suddenly, the inner voice became silent, very silent, and almost felt numb. Then it whispered again, 'Hey you, this is not a stumbling block. This is your launch pad.'

My Rugged Terrain

I remembered that element of faith had joined hands with hope, and both of them just arrived on time once again to welcome my spirits. With my spirits glowing, I found yet another venue to inspire others. 'Despite the Challenges' ®, a TV show was born.

Not sure if I was inspiring viewers of my show, or my TV show guests left me inspired every time. The fellow travelers who themselves have been through somewhat tough journeys surrounded me. They had changed their course of life with the courage and strength they possessed. The journey was filled with twist and turns at every stage, only if we can understand during the moments of trial we have been through, that we received chances to learn life with its mysterious ways and must accept it with grace.

Of all the battles I have faced, I don't know how many I've won and how many I've lost. What I remember is that I fought all of them with all my strength. I found that strength by not giving up and not giving in when facing adversity. How life just slipped away, I often wondered, remembering my childhood, my youth, my dreams for life, my journey through the jagged paths. How can one get this far walking alone?

Today, I stand proud and tall for all the opportunities I have been presented, some sour, some sweet, some bitter, some painful, some pierced my soul deep, some lifted the spirits high, so many teachers appeared from near and far at every intersection to guide me. I know now when life poured surmounting challenges in my paths, it whispered to me each time, "Where there is a will, there is a way."

Ritu Chopra

DR. FRED DiDOMENICO: Dr. Fred DiDomenico graduated chiropractic school in1987. He was inspired to help as many people as possible live the true optimal spine/optimal health lifestyle. His vision has always been to raise the consciousness of corrective chiropractic in the profession and general public around the world. He practiced for 14 years in four high volume practices. He then felt the inspiration and responsibility to create a greater impact on the profession toward spinal correction, so he founded Elite Chiropractic Coaching. Elite Chiropractic Coaching a highly powerful communication and leadership training creating the most advanced corrective chiropractic practices in the profession. As a life coach, Dr. Fred has found through coaching, a person is only as successful in their practice and life as they are as a person. Because of this, he has applied his professional self-empowerment, life coaching and leadership training to help doctors and teams release their limiting beliefs, discover, and align with their true innate power to create and completely fulfill their purpose in chiropractic and in their life. The personal growth that occurs in doctors, teams and lifetime patients in Elite Chiropractic Coaching is one of the most valuable benefits of this system in these practices and in the profession. After the passing of his wife, he developed a spiritually based life coaching system called H.E.A.L.E.D.™, which is introduced in his book called, "You Are More Powerful Than You Think," to help people in the general public discover their innate divinity, move beyond the pain of their past, discover and live their soul purpose in this life. He has a vision to raise the consciousness of people to find their soul purpose, live a chiropractic lifestyle and make the world a better place with peace and health to humanity. Please join this movement. Humanity needs you.

> FINDING STRENGTH, FINDING A PATH

H.E.A.L.E.D.

> *You don't have to know anything, be spiritual, or have any experience, if you do, great. It is not a prerequisite. ALL you need is to have an unwavering desire to discover who you are created to be and have the desire to live with this awareness and express it in your life more often than your pain. It's just that simple.*
>
> *~ Dr. Fred DiDomenico*

We sat in the doctor's office waiting for him to enter and let us know of his findings from the bone scan. She had already been through chemo and radiation from what they believed was isolated breast cancer. She sat there scared, anxious, and huddling next to me, while every second seemed like an eternity for her to get her death sentence. I was trying to instill calmness and confidence, yet I also was anticipating the avalanche of emotion that was about to come. I took some deep breaths and waited for the storm to hit. He walked in, very directly, surprisingly, almost detached. I'm sure he had this conversation often with his patients and had taught himself how to be objective, rather than sympathetic and compassionate that we are people, NOT a diagnosis. To be honest, this experience was disappointing, even frustrating. The cancer had spread throughout her body and there was nothing he could do. She immediately burst into tears. I asked the doctor to leave the room and give us a little time, as his energy in the room was not welcomed at this moment. I held her, let her cry, as I was simultaneously preparing myself emotionally and spiritually for what we were about to go through. We went home and gave her some time to process her experience that day. She decided she was giving up! As a chiropractor and natural health care provider for decades, I knew natural, holistic, health care providers she could see that have helped people just like her become cancer free. She refused again! She sat in our family room telling her kids she didn't want to live anymore.

We all BEGGED her to try, to not leave her family. In a moment, in the midst of the hurt, our conversation progressed into a heated argument. I was upset, angry, and raising my voice at her expressing my hurt and internal pain from her lack of desire to live and be healthy. This was not the first time we disagreed on this. I always say God will meet you where you are and talk to you in a language you can understand. I was a martial artist. Suddenly, in mid syllable of raising my voice in my hurt, I shockingly felt a punch to my left jaw, as if I was punched with a right hook by NO ONE standing in front of me. In fact, my head INVOLUNTARILY turned to my right, as I FELT a sore spot on my left jaw. I abruptly stopped talking consumed in total confusion.

"Did I just get punched in the face?" Then a loud, audible voice, like someone who was NOT in front of me, speaking out loud in the kitchen said to me, "Why don't you just love her the way she is?" I was stunned and shocked! I sat there in total amazement, then calmly said to myself, "I never thought of that." So incredible, sometimes we NEVER think of always loving unconditionally. It was a pivotal, life-changing epiphany of my life, TOTAL ACCEPTNCE, no matter what! Unconditional love and acceptance. What a concept! She was looking in total confusion because I suddenly stopped raising my voice at her. I looked at her and said, "OK! Ok, I'll support you (to her death)." I realized at that moment she was on her own journey with God. She was CHOOSING to leave her body now.

I decided, I will love her unconditionally to her last breath, and that's what I did. She taught me unconditional love! It was one of the most powerful, impressionable, unforgettable healing experiences and gifts in

H.E.A.L.E.D.

my whole life! I thank her for that. Four months after that day, cancer was overtaking her body. She was very thin, less than 100 lbs. Her energy was very low and diminishing. The life force in her eyes was slowly fading, and it was easy to see she was struggling to hold on. She lay in the bathtub, calmly, as she was lovingly describing her requests for her soon to be, life celebration service. She was very certain about what she wanted, although I was going to plan something even greater for her and her family!

All of a sudden, in a split moment, she started sobbing loudly. Not just crying, SOBBING aloud! Suddenly, startled and confused, I asked her with deep concern, compassion, and empathy, "What's wrong?" Her next sentence shocked me and changed my life forever. She said, "I don't know if I did what I was meant to do in this life." Hearing this overwhelming sadness and despair, overtook my body.

It felt so heavy and immediately, emotionally weighed me down. It was almost too heavy and sad to carry. I can't describe this feeling in words. The shocking irony was, in contrast, I felt gratitude that I WAS living my purpose. It was the oddest, simultaneous darkest, dark feeling, coexisting with the brightest light. It was like feeling heaven and hell at the same time.

Then this powerful feeling of unwavering, deep, heartfelt conviction and determination began to rise in my body like mercury in a heated thermometer. The very next moment a VERY LOUD voice in my head, with the highest passion, conviction, determination, and soulful, deep intent, as loud as someone speaking loudly in the same room said, "NO ONE in my life will EVER say those words to me again!" I meant it DEEPLY in EVERY CELL of my body and in my soul. Little did I know, at that moment, those words were the initiation of my next, massive, life-changing purpose.

Three weeks later, at 3 am, on November 28, 2004, in the middle of the night, I awoke next to this morbid death moan emerging from deep inside her. She was dying now. That morbid moan was truly the sound of death releasing her last breath of life force. I was begging her to just let go. "Stop fighting." I felt this deep yearning, begging her to stop her own pain, and stop the pain we ALL felt watching her die every day for months. This is the end! At this moment. She was still insisting on not giving up, and still fighting a battle she already lost. Her body was completely wasted away, she weighed maybe 80 lbs., just a skeleton. All strength in her was gone, not even enough life energy to make a flinch. After the sound of constant moaning filling the house for the next 12 hours, at 3pm, I noticed it was suddenly silent. I was right next to her and the sudden silence could cut through steel. I reached over and took her carotid and radial pulse. NOTHING! NO PULSE! NO LIFE! I had never felt no pulse. I was a doctor. NEVER had I felt no pulse. The shock of no pulse with my wife, shockingly hit me like a ton of bricks fell on me. She was gone!

This MASSIVE TIDAL WAVE of emotion suddenly wanted to explode out of me. ALL my pain, sorrow, anger, hurt, love, frustration, all my emotions wanted to explode out of me in loud cries with a wave of tears flooding like a tidal wave, yet I had to push it down. Our agreement was for me to call her family so they could view her, say "Goodbye," so they could see her one last time before she was cremated, her choice. I COULDN'T cry now. Pushing that tidal wave down deep inside me, that felt like a lifetime of pain and tears, was BY FAR, the MOST DIFFICULT task I have ever had to perform.

I pulled determination from somewhere SO DEEP inside me, I can't tell you how I even did it. There was no thought, just extreme will power. I stopped the tears by fighting, pushing and willfully forcing them down as I made those calls to her family. It felt like I was trying to shut down an uncontrollable fire hose. Then finally, I closed them off. I pushed those tears SO HARD, SO DEEP inside me, it took me two years before the first tear would ever be released. I made the calls and her family came to give her their last respects.

As I saw her dead body in our bed, I could feel her presence about five feet above her body just floating and watching us. She felt calm and free of her dead, lifeless, diseased body. Eight hours later, at 11pm, the coroner arrived to take her now stiff lifeless body away. I picked up her body and put her in the body bag. I zipped up the bag, and as I zipped it up, pausing over her face, I looked at her one last time, intently and said my last heartfelt, sad "Goodbye." Then I zipped it over her face. It was done!

H.E.A.L.E.D.

After she passed, part of me went with her in that body bag. Part of me died with her. For the next four months, I was sick in bed four times, it was hard to be in my house, and I was running from myself and those buried tears I couldn't cry out and release. My eyes didn't cry, but my heart didn't stop crying.

Finally, four months after her passing, I had a moment of presence, a reality check, and realized I was slowly killing myself. That was it! I HAD to move on! I began this very intense spiritual journey to become the most amazing man, the man God created me to be, to fulfill my purpose and meet the most amazing woman that would only have an amazing man. I was tired of pain in relationships and life. I just wanted peace, joy, and love. I began an even more intense spiritual journey to evolve.

Five years later, a life-changing event happened while I was sitting at my kitchen table. I was in a very creative mode, writing a chiropractic manual, and suddenly, involuntarily, the acronym H.E.AL.E.D. fell in my lap. A deluge of visions, one after another, began appearing in front of my eyes, like a movie trailer playing right in front of me, giving me premonitions of the life-changing impact it was going to become. I had no idea what each letter was supposed to be, yet I knew it was the most powerful, unique emotional and spiritual healing system for people to discover and LIVE their soul purpose. THIS was a result of that pivotal moment, five years earlier, when my wife was in the bathtub and those POWERFUL, CONVICTED words spoke to me, "NO ONE in my life will EVER say those words to me again!"

Everything came into place at this moment. Have you ever felt like your whole life converged into meaning in one moment? Like every challenge, every blessing, every question you've had, and every relationship, all of a sudden made sense, leading you to that moment?

This is what I experienced. It all became clear, this is what I'm supposed to do for the rest of my life, help people realize Who they REALLY Are, who they are created to be, everything in your life happened for a reason, INCLUDING your worst pain. That it was all Divinely orchestrated to bring you to your purpose. I had to live it first to teach it. Then I thought, "Now what am I going to do?" Isn't that the question that challenges us the most? We get a vision/inspiration, and we have NO IDEA HOW we are going to do it.

I just started writing the book. I had to LIVE IT, to WRITE IT! The wild ride in this transformation began. While living it to write it I had several very intense, life-changing spiritual experiences that enlightened me with wisdom and knowledge to help transform others. This next story is one of them.

One morning I woke up with this deep inspiration to know my Self, my spirit, who God created me to be innately, the spirit inside me. I was reciting this phrase with great, heart-felt intent, "I now vibrate to the energy of love, illumination, bliss, and infinite peace." I saw this in a book by Wayne Dyer and I was intensely focused on feeling these words in my body. I sat down with my head in my hands repeating this mantra over and over with increasing intensity, feeling my body vibration rising.

All of a sudden, I looked up and my spirit stepped out of my body, turned around and faced me. My translucent Self was staring back at me and looked just like me. It was my spirit. I was almost too out of my mind to even be surprised or shocked. My spirit looked directly into my eyes and said to me telepathically, "This is who you are." My body and mind were willingly under command of my spirit. I immediately acknowledged my Self with a head nod, "Yes." That wasn't enough. My spirit said, "Look again," knowing I didn't really understand. I looked again more intently and focused. I was definitely looking at my translucent spirit with my face, eyes, and body. It hit me deeper and I felt the confirmation in my body as I observed. I was looking at my Self. I nodded again, and my spirit nodded back. Then my spirit proceeded to walk toward me, right into me again and there I was, sitting just like I started. Did That REALLY HAPPEN? I knew it did! I asked to know myself, and my Self appeared! This began the first letter of H.E.A.L.E.D., "H – Honor God Within Yourself." We are Divine FIRST! We are NOT our body. We live in our body and use it as a vehicle to have human/physical experiences to evolve and fulfill our soul purpose. I was given this experience to know it within myself, so I can have the confidence to help you know we ALL are ALL the same.

H.E.A.L.E.D.

In the book, "You Are More Powerful Than You Think," and online coaching system, youaremorepowerful.com, introducing and guiding through the six steps of H.E.A.L.E.D., you too can experience and expand your consciousness, have internal peace, know your soul purpose, why you are here in this life, and live a more fulfilling, purpose-driven, amazing life. "Just Follow the Steps." You don't have to know anything, be spiritual, or have any experience, if you do, great. It is not a prerequisite. ALL you need is to have an unwavering desire to discover who you are created to be and have the desire to live with this awareness and express it in your life more often than your pain. It's just that simple.

It has changed my life, and the lives of hundreds of people and brought them a new, more empowered life because they know who they truly are!

Dr. Fred DiDomenico

JENNELL COOK: Jennell is a Wellness Educator specializing in her own Simple Health Test method. She is a CRA Practitioner (Contact Reflex Analysis) and holds her Ph.D. in the Philosophy of Designed Clinical Nutrition (under the grandfather clause). Jennell continued to earn her diplomas as a Clinical and Certified Hypnotherapist and Chartered Herbalist. She completed Levels 1 through 4 of Touch for Health by the Canadian Association of Kinesiology and Brain Gym. She discovered a way to combine her 30+ years of education and expertise to create her Simple Health Test method. Jennell and her mother had the incredible opportunity to learn, heal and work together. After her mother's astonishing recovery from multiple illnesses, they opened Better Health & Nutrition Centre. A popular health food store and clinic known for their unique testing method. When they lost their clinic in a fire, they went into private practice and travelled to clients' homes. They helped thousands of people, and pets, improve their health. Currently, Jennell is creating an online teaching platform using her simplified three-step approach to health. Her mini-series of books has begun, each targeting a dedicated issue and designed to make health less complicated. Included are stories, testimonials and resources that inspire and help people. Jennell is a proud mother of two amazing daughters and blessed with three beautiful grandchildren. She enjoys growing food in her beautiful gardens. She has a true passion and love for animals, and her ultimate dream is to have a hobby farm. Jennell is inspiring and acknowledged for helping others achieve their most successful health outcomes. She reminds us to never give up on ourselves. Do what we love, laugh and be playful. If it is a health-related matter, remember - when in doubt, test it out using a Simple Health Test.

FINDING STRENGTH, FINDING A PATH

BORN THIS WAY

> *A whole new world of possibilities became available when I enrolled in classes on herbalism and the healing arts.*
>
> *~ Jennell Cook*

Suddenly I woke, gasping for air. It was so hard for me to breathe; I was scared. Anxiety would start first, then turn to panic; I would run to get my mom. She would take me into the bathroom, run a hot shower and fill the room with steam. That's what we were told to do back then. I experienced many nights like this during my early years; I was born with a breathing issue. My mother was relieved we lived near a hospital. I was relieved my mom was there, so I didn't go through those times alone. We had no idea why it would happen, what caused it or when it might happen again. This wasn't something I grew out of. I started to notice I was trying to catch my breath a lot. It was almost a habit, and not because of any physical activity; I could be doing nothing at all. I never thought my life was limited; this was normal to me. Like wearing glasses, you get up and put them on without even thinking about it. I should have, though, because later, I learned this wasn't normal and never grew out of it.

I was 15 years old when I first questioned our health care system because of my mother. She was born with a mitral valve issue and suffered from multiple other illnesses. I thought she might not make it to see my graduation; her health was declining. My mother was a model patient, regularly seeing her doctors and specialists. She took all of her medications as prescribed. It had even been suggested it was all in her head and referred to a psychiatrist. The system failed her. It was complicated and scary. For her, this involved multiple appointments, referrals with long wait times, invasive methods and treatments, painful procedures, and many different medications with numerous side effects. We needed a different kind of help. Then along came Charles Potter, an herbalist. I had no idea what an herbalist was, but somehow, I knew that he could help, and he did. He used a type of energy work, healing, and vitamins. Nothing we had ever seen or heard of before. He showed my mother where the imbalances were in her body. I explained how balance could return by giving the body what it needs to correct itself. Her medications were slowly reduced as specialized nutrition was used in its place. We were utterly amazed.

I recall the very first time Charles helped me. One night, I had another episode of gasping for air. Once again, I ran to my mother for help. It was late in the evening, dark outside; mom was in the living room when I ran in crying. Without hesitation, she called Charles. There was no appointment necessary; he said to bring me over right away. Charles opened the door and directed us to his office. I'm sure he could see how afraid I was and that I needed help. I anticipated many questions and paperwork, but instead, I was brought right in to lay on his table. He placed his hand, his 'healing hand,' he called it, over my throat. My breathing slowed down in only a few moments; then, a certain calmness came over me. I had no idea what had just happened. Never before has this been my experience. Charles showed me that health did not have to be so complicated and scary. I laid there for a while, resting, while Mom and Charles completed the necessary paperwork. I began to wonder why everyone does not do this. If other doctors knew about it, lives would drastically change. Charles asked me to stand up to show us a few things. He demonstrated how the energy from using his healing hand could help balance my thyroid. This allowed me to calm down, and my breathing returned to normal. I was grateful to have been shown this valuable technique to use anytime. Charles taught me through his knowledge and guidance what health could look like. He worked with my mother to assist her with everything from exhaustion to pain. Charles taught us how an unhealthy diet or lifestyle contributed to her issues. He showed us tools that gave us a straightforward way to know what was helping or hurting. I learned so much from this kind man. I loved to hear his stories and hung on to his every word. A whole new world of possibilities became available when I enrolled in his class. Mom and I followed in his footsteps with herbalism and the healing arts. This continued to light up our path to wellness.

Sadly, the day came when Charles retired to a nursing home but not before introducing us to another specialized technique in energy and nutrition founded by Dr. Versendall. We began our next journey with this remarkable man and his brilliant method. He detected the lung injury I had been born with and helped me recover using his specialized nutrition. Once again, it was proven how health could be using the correct method. Over the next decade, we continued travelling to other parts of the world, attending workshops, seminars, and classes. We studied, practiced, and perfected our craft. I am so grateful for the two amazing men who taught us so much. Not only did they save my mother and help me, but they gave us the skills to help hundreds of people in thousands of situations. It gave me the ability to help my children who faced health crises that could have turned out very badly!

It was a terrible time in my life, my marriage had been falling apart, and my young daughter was struggling. The family drama affected our home life. On top of that, she was being bullied at school, and cyberattacks began. I couldn't even begin to explain the mental torture she endured. She was so stressed from dealing with other children, parents, multiple schools and even the police. Counselling helped but was not nearly enough. She suffered intensely, and I was worried. Having not experienced this myself, I couldn't understand what she was going through. I turned to the only thing I knew. I discovered a weakness in an area of the brain that controls emotions like depression and found what nutrition could help strengthen it. Steadily she became better, stronger, and excelled like never before.

Hearttalks

Her life journey is now full of possibilities with confidence and knowledge. There is nothing more precious to me than my children and grandchildren. I will never forget the day my oldest daughter was in labour. I eagerly waited for the news and all of the details about my soon-to-be granddaughter. While reading a book to keep my mind occupied and relaxed, I received a frightening text message. My daughter was in trouble! There were complications, with a strong possibility she could bleed to death. She explained that the hospital and staff did everything within their ability to help control and stop the bleeding; oral, IV, topical, nothing helped. Once again, I did the only thing I knew. I tested, found the weakness, and determined the nutrition she needed. At that time, visitors and delivery of items were not allowed. Even if I could see her, I lived two hours away, and she needed help immediately! Over the years, I learned to do remote energy healing. My daughter and I successfully used this in the past. I sent a text telling her we would use that same technique. I reassured her we were powerful together and we would fix this. I explained what nutrition was needed to support the weakness found. We visualized the nutrition going into her body and used our healing hands to balance the weakness. The bleeding stopped.

One might argue that this was a coincidence, and yes, that could be true. Then the next wave hit, an additional text with more panic from my daughter. My beautiful granddaughter would be taken from her within the hour if her blood sugar did not improve. Once again, we got back to work, this time on my grandbaby, whom I had not even met yet. Using the same incredible method, we repeated the process. Thankfully, my grandbaby recovered with no further issues.

The only thing closer to my heart than my children would be my pets; I see them as my family too. I have been the proud owner of many dogs, cats, rabbits, rats, guinea pigs and a ferret with many four-legged fur grandbabies! Since a child, my love for animals has been constant, with a need to serve and protect them. The knowledge and skills we developed were not just for people but for animals too.

Over the years, we helped heal injuries, eyesight, poisoning, hearing loss, hip dysplasia, allergies, and so much more. Let me introduce you to Jade, the six-week-old kitten thrown from a moving car. Miraculously,

Born This Way

her worse physical injury was road rash, but the mental trauma she suffered was heartbreaking. This beautiful kitten was extremely antisocial, nervous, and afraid of loud noises. She would often hide inside a box spring mattress in her new loving home. In addition to dealing with her emotional state, she suffered from chronic diarrhea. For several months we worked patiently correcting each weakness. As Jade matured, she revealed her long, fluffy coat with a foxlike tail. She was stunning. Then one day, her fur began to fall out, look dull and mangy. The testing indicated it was a blanket she had been sleeping on. She was given a new blanket, and her coat returned to its beautiful state. Today Jade is a happy, social, healthy adult cat living peacefully with her same loving family.

Our family's health struggles have been our biggest blessing and my biggest lessons. Today, my mother is thriving in her 80s, working full time and dedicating her life to helping others. My journey has begun a new chapter shifting from practitioner to educator. With a vision to help bring clarity to the overwhelming number of products on the market today and conflicting health information. I am passionate about sharing our stories and teachings through an online course and mini-series of books. This has brought a significant purpose to my life and shown me a deeper sense of what I was born to do.

Jennell Cook

JUDY LEE: Who is Judy Lee? She is a woman who has faced adversity head on and has come through. Having lost a sister and cousin to breast cancer, she knew the perils of the disease and never considered it to be her path in life. In 2016 that changed and she had to confront the decision of mastectomy or live. The choice seems obvious yet the struggle to reach the decision and live a life as an "unnatural" woman was real. She found healing throughout the excruciating pain of recovery and insomnia through art merging her love for photography and new technology which assisted her in being in the zone while being in pain. She wants to educate and make a difference in bringing awareness to the variety of experiences one may go through as they deal with breast cancer and mastectomy.

She lives in California and is working on the next book in this series as well as a book based on her sister's life as pioneer in aviation in Jamaica and a casualty of breast cancer. Judy Lee speaks on how to soar to new heights in the face of adversity. Judy Lee has a BA in Radio Television Film Production from California State University, Northridge.

FINDING STRENGTH, FINDING A PATH

I CRY

> *There is healing after cancer. You may be wondering if that is truly possible. Well, I can tell you from my own experience life is filled with before and after. Before cancer, it was something I was not going to get. Then there was the diagnosis, the reconciliation and struggles and now there is life.*
>
> *~ Judy Lee*

There is healing after cancer. You may be wondering if that is truly possible. Well, I can tell you from my own experience life is filled with before and after. Before cancer, it was something I was not going to get. Then there was the diagnosis, the reconciliation and struggles and now there is life.

Her last church service was Easter Sunday, 23 April 2000. Saturday night before going home, I went into Yola's room. She lay quietly on the bed, television flickering in the background. She looked up from her gaze and I saw the tired look and a bit of defeat in her eyes.

Yola – come for you tomorrow for church?

I saw her thinking about how she was feeling and if she had the strength to go and picking at her chin, a chronic habit that developed during her last stage of cancer.

Yes, come.

Hearttalks

Ok, I will see you in the morning as I leaned forward and stroked her round fuzz filled bald head. *I just love the feel of your hair now Yola, I just love how downy soft if feels* and then kissed her on the forehead. I drove home alone, as my son, who was 10 wanted to sleep over with his Auntie, and I was happy thinking about the Easter service in the morning and calculating the time that I would need. I needed time to drive from my house to Mommy's about five minutes. Then go into the house and walk her to the car should take about 10 minutes as she was moving more slowly; go back inside and get the wheelchair, put the wheelchair in the trunk would take another three minutes; drive to Church, get the wheelchair out of the trunk and open it up would take 15 minutes; help her out of the car and into the wheelchair then wheel her into the service and I may have to fix her wig and just a pause to tell her she looked beautiful, would take another five minutes. I added on an extra 30 minutes to my wake-up time so that I could be punctual and get her to the Easter morning service on time. Traveling with Yola had become adding on time to make sure you arrived on time. It was about patience and moving slowly. It was about caring and realizing when she was tired and needed to take more frequent breaks, and it was about honoring her request to be treated with dignity and not be treated as an invalid.

I then thought about how grateful I was to be sharing another special time with my sister and tears brimmed over my lids, slowly rolling down my cheeks as the thought of her getting weaker by the day. Her body, once strong and full, had become frail and bony with her back hunched over like the Hunchback of Notre Dame with the legion protruding down the spine where a tumor was growing and becoming more painful day by day. My mind's eye saw the pain that shadowed her eyes, yet Yola remained strong and focused on completing her last days with us in dignity and valor, not complaining about the pain or her circumstance. What a woman! How does she do it? How does she continue to go on? If it were me, I'd be gone by now. I could not stand the agony or deterioration of my body. I wish I were more like my sister.

Sunday morning came and I got up to chauffer her to Easter Sunday service. When I arrived at the house it was quiet. Everyone was still sleeping or had not stirred for the day. I went into Yola's room and saw

I Cry

her sitting on the beige recliner beside her bed with her face in her hand with her eyes closed.

Yola are you alright?

She looked up slowly and saw me. It took her a few seconds to adjust to see me and then she responded.

Yes, I'm just tired.

Are you sure you want to go? I asked softly as I moved closer to her picking up her dress from the ground beside her.

After a brief pause, quietly she said, *yes. Yes, I want to go.*

Just take your time, Yola as she stretched out her hand for me to help her to her feet. She was clad in her marina and her thin body was that of an old woman, shriveled and aging. Everything was sagging on her. I held onto what I thought would have been hands, but it was skin and bones. It was my sister. I looked at her and what was feeling in that moment I knew I had experienced it before. And then it hit me.

The love that oozes out of a mother's body with the birth of her child is like no other I had been told many times over the years. My son was now 10 and I feel love for him no matter what. That unconditional love that seeps through each pore, each cell, each fiber of your body is unmatched. And I was feeling this for this imposter who was standing holding onto me as I helped dress her for church. After I finished dressing her, she sat in exhaustion. Turning away from her, eyes wet with tears wanting to overflow, I walked to the dresser and said, *which wig you want to put on today. It is Easter Sunday and you have to look pretty.*

Yes, give me that one, as she lifted her finger ever so slightly to point to the one she desired. As I picked it up and brushed it, I thought of how much I love her. How much my heart was filling up with the memories of being there for her now that she needed me? I am happy to have resolved our issues and to be a part of her life now. It was a miracle and I was experiencing absolute love, joy and compassion mixed into a bowl called Yola. It was euphoric. It was the best feeling I had had since my son was born. I loved her and there was no longer any question in my mind what I would do for my sister. And then in an instant I got sad again. Why did I wait so long to reconcile with her? What did I gain from all of those lost years and time spent with the vibrant, alive person who was now dying? Why did I waste so much time? And the tears came. I couldn't hold them back. I tried desperately to stop and when Yola looked up she saw me.

Don't cry Judy, don't cry. I am going to be with God and it will be all right. I promise you that you will be okay. Here give me the wig, she said and tried to lift her arms to take it but couldn't. She started to cough. I reached over and put the wig on her head and in an instant, she told me to take it off.

I will put it on when we get closer. I'm hot and she reached up to have me help her stand to go to Church. We arrived at Church of the Valley late as it had taken us longer to leave the house than I had calculated. I had not anticipated her being tired and moving really slowly. I had not anticipated her feeling sick yet still wanting to go.

We entered the Church through the front, I rolled the wheelchair towards the front, and sat next to her as a member moved over for me to be with her. I joined in on the hymn being sung while finding the page in the hymnal for Yola. I placed the book in her hand and she held it firmly. She sat and looked towards the front of the Church and I saw her moving her lips to the song. After the song, she closed her eyes and tears ran down her cheeks. I watched and I too started sharing those tears. I then looked ahead and listened in silence to the Minister's words. Yola sat and participated with her eyes closed most of the service. She was there physically, yet I know she was having a heart-to-heart talk with God asking for his mercy and help in making her journey easier. I felt she was asking for guidance on how to leave the children and asking what was her purpose in these final moments. I think her questions and her desire to be in God's house on Easter Sunday when Jesus rose from the dead was for her calming, joyous, and merciful. She was at one with her maker, the Almighty. She did participate in communion as I took the bread for her and put it in her mouth. She held the cup and shakily held it as was the tradition in the church. She drank the wine with everyone else and I know she was touched by the joy she felt being with the congregation.

After church she did not want to stay and motioned for me to take her home quickly.

I Cry

What's up Yola?

Not feeling good. Want to throw up. Just get me home.

I helped her into the car and some other church members helped me put the chair in the car.

Bye Yola, they said, and all she could do was close her eyes and nod with a small smile on her face.

She's not feeling well. I'm taking her home.

Go with God. Bye Yola, they said again.

That memory captured mine as I sat in my home, curled up, with tears flowing down my cheeks, sitting in shock on the recliner after I heard the words from my doctor, *you have cancer and you need a mastectomy*. I never heard the words you need a mastectomy. That came the following week after another conversation with him. I had called my other sister Mitz and told her and she said, *Juds you will need to get through this one so the children can see a different outcome.* Yola had died leaving behind two small children and my son was 10 when she died.

You are going to get through this became the echoing theme from everyone around me. It was a curse, a burden, and a future that I lived into every day.

Having witnessed my sister's death and subsequently that of my cousin, both from breast cancer, my desire was to have a different outcome. I wanted to go about it in a non-traditional way, and my son and family were not so inclined. Everyone I knew told me just do the mastectomy and move on. I also heard, if you want to get any type of breast cancer, this is it as it is the one with the least effects. It is DCIS, Ductal Carcinoma In-situ. Everyone, including the doctor said that mastectomy was my only option.

When I awoke from the fog I was in, I contacted my herbalist and went for a consultation. His view is that cutting out any type of cancer leaves the possibility of the cancer getting into the bloodstream and spreading, so it was important to not do the surgery and for me to be on a regime of vitamins, minerals, and a different diet. I started that immediately as I continued following doctors' orders for more testing and getting the information necessary to decide mastectomy or not.

Hearttalks

I consulted with a friend, a breast cancer surgeon and when he reviewed my results, he said, the doctors were correct. I asked if I could wait for an additional 4 months, so that I could see some results from the change of diet and minerals.

The answer from him and another set of doctors was in short – *are you crazy?*

I now had to confront what was life going to be like with losing my breasts. I was hopeful that the tumor would shrink with the changes in my dietary habits and if that happened, I could delay having surgery and I would be an example of going opposite to what the health professionals wanted. I wanted to be that one!

The reality soon sank in. It wasn't shrinking and time was running out to make a decision. After countless doctor's visits, testing, probing, poking, feeling, touching it became obvious to me that I had to make a decision. The fear was great. The trepidation real. I was scared and unwilling to face the fact that I was going to lose my breast. I started to look at pictures of women with mastectomies. I researched, and googled, and asked questions of friends who had gone through the process. All the pictures and stories did not give me hope. I saw women after women with scars across their chests. I remembered my sister's scars and her journey. I saw women with tattoos, I saw slender women, tall women, white women. I did not see me. I did not see a mature, heavy-set Black woman who was single and had just started to the process of exploring dating after all these many years. I did not see short women with dark skin in pictures. I did not see what women like me looked like and I could not envision what I would look or could look like after surgery much less after surgery and reconstruction.

Talk about reconstruction! Perky breasts. What size do you want your breasts? It's like getting a boob job for free! You are so lucky you will get to have new breasts. That is what people think this is about. For some people this is their dream and wish. Some see it as a way to create a new body with all their desires met. For me, it was the worst nightmare come to life. I had the breast I had that fit my body at my age had after nursing a child. I had the breasts I had and didn't know how to size them. I wore the bra the way I wore a bra and most times, as women

I Cry

know, we wear ill-fitting bras. How was I to decide? And from this came an obsession to look at women's breasts. I would see women, and trying to match body type to mine and see what size fit. It was for me embarrassing and painful. This is more work than I wanted. I just wanted this whole ordeal to end.

I wanted the DIEP Flap reconstruction. The simplest way to describe it, is you take the fat and skin from the lower abdomen and that then becomes the breast with all the blood vessels and it feels like your body. That was what I wanted, not silicone implants as those are changed every 10 years and that was not for me. Plus, can you imagine a wrinkled old body looking like a raisin with two coconuts on top. That was not an image I wanted for myself.

I spoke to the plastic surgeon, this tall, very handsome "childlike" looking surgeon. He was cute and that made the visit tolerable. He is speaking with me and I say, *well doc* very lightheartedly, *can I get the keyhole, nipple sparing surgery*. He looks up at me wondering why I am asking this of him. I had already done my research; my surgeon friend had told me what to ask for. *Well, we don't do that here*, he says. I looked at him and he continues, *we do the basic cut which is from side to side of the breast*. My eyes widened in horror. That is exactly what I did not want to have this ungodly scar across my chest. I then looked at him in the eyes and said, *"well, if you can't do a nipple sparing keyhole cut, then I will take my cancer and go somewhere else!"* His eyes widened and I could see the shock on his face. He was flabbergasted that someone would say something like that to him. I kept looking at him. He says, *hold on, let me measure you*. Then he preceded to measure my breast and the nipple and said, *"we can do it and I am not sure we will be able to save the nipple as the tumor is too close to it*. I said, *okay then, go ahead and take the nipples*. In that moment I felt for the first time in control of my destiny with this disease.

I couldn't see me ever being in a relationship again. For me every woman's body I saw looked gross. I was angry, sad and hopeless. I did not want to live. Why couldn't I have died instead of Yola?

Over the course of the journey from hearing the call to today, what I do know is that the journey of breast cancer is unique to each individual. It is a personal journey. I healed by taking charge of my care, my

Hearttalks

decisions. I asked a lot of questions. I had a team of people around me whom I confided in. They were my support, my everything. These people were for me, who I was for my sister. They were my advocates in love and life. This story continues as I live, grateful for the lessons learned, blessed with memories of my sister, Yola who started this conversation of breast cancer. Grateful for showing perseverance, dignity, and love so that I now get to contribute to women going through the journey. I get to be a guide for my family, showing there is light that can be visible in darkness. Out of all of this, I am now an author and artist. You never know where your pains and hurts will take you. Live life to the fullest each and every day! F-Cancer!

Judy Lee

JESSICA FLAGIELLO: By day, Jessica Flagiello works as a sales and hospitality manager at various jobs; however, she imagines being a superhero at night in Toronto, Canada. She expertly crafts writings for operational strategies and innovative marketing plans for many companies to grow. She trains entrepreneurs in mind-setting techniques and also coaches soccer. When Jessica is not immersed working on leadership development presentations and outreach projects on a local and international level, you can find her meditating to feel grounded and happy. She practices a spiritual lifestyle with the Hare Krishna community where she has started several initiatives and serves on different programs. Her personal mantra is, "Keep moving forward." Her inspiration, encouragement, and appreciation has helped numerous people worldwide find their path that enriches and uplifts them. With her witty humour, authenticity, enthusiasm, and depth of wisdom that captures hearts and minds, she continues to improve with courage, passion, and a lot of laughter along the way. Jessica loves spending time with her family and friends and getting into trouble with her nephews. She enjoys traveling the world with an itinerary, cooking, hiking in nature, star gazing, visiting museums, and playing sports. She is obsessed with collecting books, postcards from her trips, listening to music, and learning new things to master as she attempts to multitask. Jessica loves meeting new people and runs an international group called Connected Souls, which brings together positive like-minded compassionate individuals to feel enlivened. One of Jessica's dreams is to be a motivational speaker as she believes we can all make an impact by empowering the potential of others through connection and love. She co-authored a chapter entitled "Continue Courageously to be Empowered" in the book *From Bottom to Top*. You can connect with her on: Facebook: Jessica Flagiello,

Instagram: jessicaflag,
Email: jessconnectedsouls@gmail.com

> FINDING STRENGTH, FINDING A PATH

FROM DESTRUCTION TO ENLIGHTENMENT

> *My consciousness considered my soul being tested by a higher power and knew the reason why everything happens is to give me the opportunity to improve and help others find their way.*
>
> *~ Jessica Flagiello*

Before you read this, please note that these words have been diluted in odium for years and are only fragments of my private expressions. I lived in obscurity because darkness was all I knew. Nevertheless, lately I have created and abide a meaningful serene life. I changed my inner aspects to improve and motivate me forward. Inevitable, my harmony was under examination to see if I truly altered.

In mid-August, there was a fight and a violent act had been committed upon me. I wish I could explain the episode, but my thoughts stumble on the page because my hand was unable to keep up. As I scrambled to put words together, they became out of sync; as it is a perfect reflection of my mind. I desire to articulate myself in length, fluidity, and depth and still, I won't admit how draining it is. I become fixated to craft flawless lines; trying to depict my emotions so other understand. I imagined living through my sorrows heroically, but this story of destruction and growth is filled with my intentions, self-discovery, and personal transformation; similar what happens to a caterpillar's journey in the cocoon state to a butterfly.

Hearttalks

I know everything happens for a reason and life tests the limits of our soul just to build character. *** I walked alone on the path; the sun shined brightly, and clouds drifted apart. Shouts intoxicated the woods as a man ran towards me. I inhaled deeply and prepared for the push. I felt hands on my shoulders as my feet stepped irregularly to ensure I wouldn't fall; yet, my balance failed. I was knocked to the ground; my body slammed incongruously, twisting to move as it adjusted from the deformed position that I landed in. My own arm wrapped around my neck; with the other hand griping the soil, trying to lift myself up. I wondered, "Am I going to die?" Due to the lack of oxygen, I laid motionless and my brain struggled to stay alive, while my body was willing something else. I disregard all the unvalued wishes I made before and only begged for air and help; but he didn't conform to my request to release me.

This assault was caused by a disagreement and I didn't plan to hurt him. I felt like a caterpillar; crawling on the earth, unnoticed and grotesque. I was fighting for life; scraping by and latching on like other insects always under scrutiny and attack. My body was trembling from the beating but my mind reinsured me that it would stop.

I needed help. I was exhausted from what I had endured but my heart was enthusiastic by love and forgiveness already. As I was covered by dirt; I envied those creatures that were not controlled by another and thought how precious, uncertain, and lack of time we have. I eliminated anger from my being or else it would have broken me and I would have been a memory.

Something astonishing happened as I looked up and saw in the distance a blue figure swaying between trees; almost cleverly keeping my attention on him so I wouldn't lose hope. Another older man appeared standing, observing, and contemplating to intervene. He too, captivated my conscious and all my energy focused on breathing. Even as my sight diminished, their outlines kept their depth of details. I felt peaceful by their presence as I assumed this was an evaluation; that impelled and guided me forward.

I aspired in those moments that my inspirational survival story might help others overcome their challenges; so I vowed to live.

From Destruction to Enlightenment

I realized my intentions were authentic and didn't want to fight as it wasn't my nature. I was confident in knowing there were people looking over me. I finally got free; as I arose and the trees, rocks, soil, and animals claimed their spots on the ground again. A loving force led me in controlling my despondency. I remained silent as I dragged myself towards a place of acceptance and refuge.

Nevertheless, I didn't find sanctuary there and it failed me. I was feeling exasperation of the annoyance of corruption to one's soul and moved on with caution. My inner vulnerabilities were exposed and I was unwilling to live in an abyss as I did everything to rise above the shadows.

The melancholy part was everyone abandoned me. It was overwhelming and pathetic no one protected me. Sadly, mental destruction overpowered me as my brain was racing, tripping, and rolling down upon its own thoughts, trying to get away from it-self. I was a master of masking my mistakes but an expert in examining others emotions.

My disgusting bodily caterpillar scurried away and left a repulsive trail that no one followed. I retreated and wandered to escape myself; how pitiful to lose oneself in oneself. I walked for hours and finally sat by the lake looking at the vast openness and perceived my life as insignificant. I was feeling alone and annihilated because my heartbroken words were out of reach but never been so loud before. I demanded silence, except the noise kept me company and soon it departed. I experienced an irrepressible bondage to loneliness and the separation amplified my longing; thus, I relinquished and cried freely. I deliberated who those men were and prayed for strength. It was vital to believe this was a trial and necessary to acquire peace and wisdom. Even feeling lost, my hope was finding an opportunity of growth in destruction; just as the caterpillar travels onwards in their journey; I too had to be compassionate in my aim of progress. Despite pain being unbearable, I had to fight for forgiveness with them. ***

Weeks later, I had insomnia because I reflected about my insecurities; questioning my perception of all my old impurities which were my only recollections of the event. By protecting my sanity, my heart couldn't rest as nightmares arrived. Anxiety crept in, causing depression and I feared an eclipse in my life would occur again. The emptiness echoed as it was ephemeral and my memoires tormented me. I could run on empty, but it is the emptiness that people feel and I never anticipated damaging myself or others. My mind kept busy; thinking its invincible but only learning its entangled by the desire to feel understood, needed and wanted.

I never imagined myself hubris, but believing that, was a sign of my immaturity protruding. Humility was the remedy to rid the nuisances of desperation. I tortured and neglected myself; being utterly alone and catastrophic by enmity. I became bewildered in isolation anguish; losing myself in the illness of destruction, fear and confinement. The caterpillar encloses itself, making a protective cocoon in order to undergo metamorphosis. I also had to enter a new stage as a pupa so I could adjust my structure and modify.

During this growth of evolution, I became fearless in emerging out of the intense pressure and couldn't forfeit on becoming conscious and appreciative. It's profound, all the hurt the heart can handle, and still hold on to hope. At that moment, I started the process of discovering features of my soul as I always had a spirituality inclination. I embraced my solitude and the notion of forgiveness started, filled, and ended my view. As I stared at my challenges; I prayed and knew immediately they would be chances to be reinvigorated with passion, patience, and empathy. I was determined to be self-aware and find purpose but I first had to find connections with myself and admiration for God.

I eagerly practiced a pious life; engaging fully as I knew all apprehensiveness I accumulated would vanish or dissolve like the outer layer of a cocoon shell. Love occupied my being and slowly I trusted the process and became happy. Similar to a caterpillar that sheltered itself to produce its wings; I absorbed my attention in learning as my need for growth outweighed the suffering. Although the evolution was treacherous; I had to fight for forgiveness with myself. ***

I couldn't allow myself to be consumed by the revulsion of the incident that had built up in my life anymore. I concluded, to move on I had to orchestrate my heart, body, spirit, and mind until they achieved the accurate affirmation. It was ambitious but acquitting empowered me

From Destruction to Enlightenment

to find compassion and understanding for others. Mental annihilation and forgiveness were the only pure agony and cure. Faith assisted me to improve by transforming doubts that use to captivate me in misery into optimistic beliefs. The influential spiritual wisdom that I gathered united, healed, and uplifted me. As I broke through layers that sealed me in; I appeared magnificent and prepared for my journey of reaching my potential. 'Courage: the weak can never forgive; forgiveness is the attribute of the strong.' (Gandhi).

I accepted everything happens for a reason and my inflicted distress gave me numerous opportunities to grow. I felt liberated; just as the butterfly emerges, cleans itself off, flaps its wings and ascends to the sky. I desired freedom to fly and share essential love as I never wanted anyone to experience that pain.

The cultivation of humility by practicing gratitude, nourished my innate ability to transcend life's circumstances and eliminate the frustration of feeling incomplete. This spiritual renewal raised my conscious and I became calm in tribulations. I understood the soul is eternally, blissful, and full of knowledge and by serving others we experience deep affection that exceeds our expectations.

I believe we all want to be happy, maintain our happiness and above all- give happiness to others as we navigate to find our own meaning in life. Associating with spiritual individuals, I continued my efforts in making progress of improving myself and feeling inner fulfillment.

My old constant perplex lamentations gave me reasons to explore my soul; allowing me to share transcendental knowledge with others so they would find the courage, tolerance, and sincerity to keep moving forward.

I transformed my bitter past into a better future and am still working on becoming the best version of myself as I didn't want to weep in weakness any longer. Like a butterfly that thought its journey ended when everything seemed disconsolate, was actually its tremendous triumph.

In recognizing my own potential, I obtained unflinching devotion as my prosperous qualities were presented when I am equanimity. As I reassessed the affair, I concluded that the two individuals in the woods that disastrous day were spiritual beings protecting me. Their manifestation revealed that I am never alone and my existence is worth everything.

Hearttalks

Realizing this, I acknowledged all turmoil situations are part of my story and a chance to transform into my most excellent self.

Forgiveness was the root of my adjustment to accelerate and amplify upwards like a butterfly. Meditating granted me the capacity to proceed peacefully towards my altitude and emulate glorious people characteristics. My aptitude shined and I soared as I rebuilt myself and wanted to make an impact on the world. I converted my energy in revolutionizing my condition of life and increasing my mindfulness and steadiness. Though my alteration was noticeable, I had to fight for forgiveness with everyone to make them understand my changes. ***

As I finished writing this narrative, I felt equipoised as the burden of carrying this memory fell away and disappeared while I prepared to lose things that held me down. The fight enraged me but I was more disappointed that it aggravated my tranquility as it was under observation and I had to learned how to deal with it.

Resources enabled me to consistently look within for realization, illuminate outward to support, rise above every occasion, and go beyond any obstacle that comes my way. My life consisted of ameliorating and managing my emotions so I would improve all aspects and keep moving forward on my journey.

This motivated me to be my best and make progress in overcoming challenges with humility. As others saw me constantly jubilant and harmonious; however, this was not always the case since only few really knew what I have gone through to achieve these accomplishments and be who I am today. I was ashamed and I encapsulated this account until it was euphony and the pain subsided.

Advancements in spirituality is assessed by the profoundness of one's genuine compassion, forgiveness, and development of being selfless. Comprehending these values, I began fully utilizing this chance to attain a purified, pleasurable, and ultimate living state. I found deep connection with myself and God as I searched my soul to identify how I can serve others.

I remembered a monk said, "How does one become a butterfly? - One must desire to fly so much that they give up being a caterpillar." Believing this statement; my nature materialized and provided me with

From Destruction to Enlightenment

relief from my suffering and the concept of a better life. I did not want to die alone in the woods; so I promised, if I lived I would be brave and graceful just as those outline people did as they gave me hope in the greatest despair.

As the caterpillar wriggles along the earth trying to detect its way at the start of their life; I sensed the same as I strolled without directions and was engrossed with calamities but my objective never wavered. The pupa entraps and recluse itself; just as I imprisoned and encircled myself in solitary to find answers to dilemmas. As an exquisite butterfly surfaces through the cocoon; I also immersed myself in the sun and freedom as I couldn't fail myself and had to reach my potential of being truly happy. My faith inspired, encouraged, and appreciated my movement forward. By learning and sharing wisdom, it allowed me to accept, understand, need, and want my own self as I aspired to develop my passions.

My growth from destruction enlightened me to live with authentic intentions, discover my real self, and transform my inner personality to find noble meaning in life. My consciousness considered my soul being tested by a higher power and knew the reason why everything happens is to give me the opportunity to improve and help others find their way. This experience aided me to become my own butterfly and promoted me to fly on my own as I advocate everything can empower someone as long as we fight, grow, and move on from it.

The possibilities are endless. This story of survival is just a chapter of my life but has given me my life to fight for. I found forgiveness for fighting but I fought for freedom to forget.

Jessica Flagiello

Michele Bell—award-winning screenwriter, fearless mother, and Grief Warrior®—translates pain into books, courses, and 1:1 retreats designed to help others through their grief and trauma. Focusing on her personal experiences and knowledge, she isn't shy about sharing her raw story. She holds a wealth of knowledge about turning pain into purpose, from losing three children, living through her brother's suicide, being bullied, living through domestic violence, and hardships people can only imagine.

Michele hopes to empower others. As a Intuitive Alchemist and Life Messenger, she works with individuals experiencing devastation and transitions theirpin into purpose. She's proud to be a mentor, teacher, and conduit and employs her authentic, down-to-earth personality to help engage and connect with others. Pain doesn't have to destroy us, but it can define us—she's chosen to turn her pain into a guiding light to help others on their life journeys. If you're reading this right now, you're here for a reason. Don't hesitate to reach out:

Contact info: TheGriefWarrior@michelecynthiabell.com

FINDING STRENGTH, FINDING A PATH

MY SON'S LOVE

> *We can't change our pasts. But we can make peace with them—and we can change our futures by taking care of our inner selves, our souls, in the present.*
>
> *-Michele Bell*

My journey in life has been anything but simple. There is no doubt about it; life's journey can be challenging, with obstacles that seem insurmountable. There have been many moments when I could have quit throughout my life experiences dealing with cancer, suicide, murder, rape, and abuse. I could have thrown in the towel and given in to the hardship life had handed me. Grief made me empowered.

I've become an expert at transforming my obstacles into opportunities and stumbling blocks into stepping stones, which has led me to become a Grief Warrior, creating a safe space to discuss the shit-show.

But it's also a place for us to share our stories, learn from each other, and heal together.

I am an Empath, manifesto, and healer. I have seen death and trauma in many forms, but my life purpose is to help others heal from grief.

Rising from the ashes of abuse, bullying, rape, sibling suicide, and parent alienation, I'm familiar with the word "trauma."

Hearttalks

I've always been smiling, pretending everything was OKAY. But at 56 years young, I have no shame in sharing. Writing has kept me alive.

It's in owning your own story that you embrace your unchangeable worth. In naming yourself the author of your own story, you can find your happy ending.

I often work with influential individuals in the entertainment industry looking for a fresh start — a new beginning to EMBRACE their life and heal forward! My customized 1:1 retreats navigate a new, higher path toward healing together. They're ready to do the inner work needed to embrace today's opportunities and become their best selves. It's an honor to work alongside them and keep their journey safe and sacred.

Let's discuss LOVE.

Love is the only thing that can drive a warrior. When I felt like giving up, when all seemed lost and impossible to overcome - there was always one hope in my heart: my love for my children. One thing that kept me fighting every day was navigating my only driven force. Love. I pushed through with love in my heart and a warrior's mentality every day. I knew I could handle anything that got in my way by placing love first. There were moments when I struggled to do so. Moments when it was hard to hold a warrior's heart. But in the end, love wins. Love always wins.

Here is my story.

Growing up, I only ever had one dream in life. I wanted to be a mother. I wanted to raise children and show them the love that I did not always receive in my home. I know I could love my children with no limits if given a chance with the purest intention of unconditional love.

Tragedy has touched me three times in my life. The first was when I lost my 18-year-old son to bone cancer. I found myself in an unspeakable situation after being sexually assaulted at work by my boss. I lost my third pregnancy to his violent physical abuse. Being a single mom with no child support was mentally challenging, but I wouldn't change my journey for anything. I am a survivor.

My Son's Love

Raising my children has been my biggest accomplishment. As a single mother, I had to balance motherhood and work. I had to provide for my children no matter what life had thrown my way, including free-style visitation with their father. That was a nightmare. The parent alienation was mentally abusive; they came home emotionally scorned every weekend. The entire family was negative from the moment I started dating my ex-husband, so it was expected, but very sad.

As the years went by, Nicky and I became inseparable. It was easy, flowing warmly. His sister Bianca was a bit of a rebel - ignited by the chaos. So I guess you could say I loved being in my son's presence because it was simplistic. The bond that Nicky and I shared was all I needed to motivate me through all the difficult moments. He kept me in alignment. His energy was that powerful!

Life as a single mother is hard enough. But it becomes ten times harder when you are targeted. I've found my energy triggers low vibrations, but then we have the simplistic energies that supersede those moments in celebration. I am forever learning. It feels good to own it.

I was confident that love would be enough to keep me safe, but the enemy had unique plans for me. When malevolence knocked on my door and tried to trick me with a false sense of hope, I looked up at the stars, which reminded me of rejuvenation of self —knowing what you're fighting against, there's no way possible of winning without divine help!

When my son was diagnosed, I knew my life would change forever. Although life threw me another curveball, I knew those struggles were minuscule compared to the vortex I was about to enter. The source of my joy and strength was in danger, and as his mother, it was my quest to give it all. I got to get us throughout this battle.

Nicky was playing in a basketball game and watching the teams playing hard and having fun from the bleachers. Nicky loved basketball, and I loved watching him play. As my son dribbled the ball up the court and tried to drive to the hoop, another team player attempted to steal the ball. During the skirmish, the player from the other team kicked my son in the leg. Nicky dropped to the court in pain, holding his leg.

After a few seconds, I jumped over the bleachers, running over the other parents. Comforting Nicky as the players swirled around us playing the game. The other team player grabbed the ball and scored. I was in shock. No one came over to help us. Nicky got up and took one for the team, literally.

What first seemed to be a somewhat typical sports injury quickly evolved into our worst nightmare. The kick that caused my son to drop to the court turned out to be the catalyst for Ewing's Sarcoma, a rare form of bone cancer. What many do not realize is that a run-of-the-mill injury to the bone or soft tissue surrounding the bones in your leg can be the cause sarcoma to grow. In Nicky's case, his injury on the basketball court began a five-year battle with this sporadic form of cancer in my son's bones, immediately spreading to both lungs.

At the time of Nicky's diagnosis, I was working two jobs to cover our needs. I worked long hours, so I could not spend as much time with my children as I would have liked, but I knew that to provide for my children, I had to make sacrifices. The love that I felt for my children motivated me to work constantly to make sure that I could give the best life for them despite the lack of support from their father. The constant brutal bantering went on for years, even after Nicky died in 2005.

When my son's treatment began in the hospital, I asked my boss to leave work early to sit with Nicky at the hospital. I figured my employers would understand my situation. It is not every day that a mother must take extra time off to be with her terminally ill child. However, I was wrong. My employers used my request as grounds for termination. They fired me the next day.

Not long after losing my job, I could not afford our house. I attempted to apply for housing help from the Eastchester housing community. I failed to pay for my home, so we became homeless. We moved into the local YMCA until I scored a commission to get us through the following year.

During this time, I was doing what I could to provide for my children. Working from the hospital, no one knew I had a sick child. But I created a stream of income despite my situation. My clients were not aware of my struggle. While I didn't have a home of my own, I worked incredibly hard to help people buy and sell their houses. I knew I had to

My Son's Love

do what I could to provide for us while not jeopardizing the time I had with my son.

My son spent five years receiving treatment and battling cancer. Throughout that entire time, I fought with every fiber to do what was best for him. Grateful for every opportunity that came my way. I am manifesting through faith, hope, and love. It's in unlocking self-discovery that we create our OWN maps for healing. I believe that you have everything you need to find the answers within yourself. However, sometimes it takes a robust constitution.

After five years of battling Ewing's Sarcoma, my son Nicky transitioned. With such a rare form of bone cancer, there was only so much that could be done for my son. He fought hard until the end, but his spirit was exhausted. It has been almost two decades since my son passed away. I still miss his presence every day. I live through the love I once knew.

Even after all my struggles and hardship, I still know one thing to be true. Love conquers all. The love that I shared with my son during his life was enough to show me that love wins, even at the hardest of times. Through the hate, pain, financial struggles, and battle with cancer, I know that love will always come out on top.

Of course, we will never let go. And we don't need to. But we can move forward with our grief and pivot into a new life and a new chapter of purpose. It is a journey of honoring our loved ones and letting them guide us to a life of divine intention, healing, and purpose.

It all starts with the choice to embrace, or what I like to call, the 7 Stages of Grief, a mini journal workbook I created after producing my first award-winning story, A Son's Gift.

EMBRACE

EXPRESS | MEDITATE | BE PRESENT | REJUVENATE| AWAKEN |CONNECT| EAT HEALTHY

These TOOLS are laid out and intuitively within my course to help you shift from resistance to embracing and pivot from pain to purpose.

Hearttalks

If my experience has taught me one thing, it is that I am a warrior. When fueled by love, I know I can shatter any barrier that stands in my way. I have a warrior's heart. Through a lifetime of struggle, I earned it. I worked countless hours, sacrificed so much, and stood in the face of hate with love in my heart, ready to do anything I needed to do to keep my children safe. When the world tried to push me down, I stood tall and fought back. I shielded my children from the world's evils, and I used my warrior energy to fight back.

Single motherhood is hard. Having your child be diagnosed with cancer is hard. Losing your job is hard. Working from your sick child's bedside and creating a new way to live is hard. Coping with chaos and loneliness is brutal. I also knew that my warrior's heart could overcome it all. Love always wins.

When you love someone as much as I loved my children, it's difficult to move past their non-existence. Grief seems like a looming shadow whose only goal is to hold you down. When we realize that the love within us is stronger than grief, we can defeat the shadow and let our light shine through. Instead of being lost, love helps us find the right path.

Love is all I know. Life moving with has ushered in the most supportive friendships. I believe our loved ones are a conduit in helping our brokenness find its way. Without authentic friendships, you might as well be alone. I can honestly say today; I feel ALIVE again.

No two grief journeys are the same, so my 1:1 retreats are tailored to my client's human design. I often work as a grief consultant in schools, prisons, and other formats. High-profile lawyers hire me to assist and uplift their clients in traumatic situations. Together, we create a magical formula to begin the journey to self. Everyone deserves the chance to heal — to pivot with purpose. And I'm here to do just that.

In life, you had two choices: to retreat or to renew. Choose to renew. Knowing that you could manifest anything you want too can be an amazingly amazing journey. Honor your soul with a complete awe of EMBRACE and MAGIC.

I could take my pain and pivot with purpose. I moved through my grief and could find fulfillment in helping others. This path is likely for

My Son's Love

everyone who has experienced a loss in their life. You must keep moving forward and let your love and the love of the one you lost shine bright.

All our lives, we're taught to resist —to resist the change. To resist pain. To resist discomfort. When we accept the things we cannot change and choose to do the things that would make our loved ones proud, we find purpose. Your past can lead you to your purpose. Your pain can become your fuel to embody and fulfill that purpose.

Rising from the ashes of abuse, bullying, rape, sibling suicide, and parent alienation, I'm familiar with the word "trauma."

I've always been smiling, pretending everything was OKAY. But at 56 years young, I have no shame in sharing. Writing has kept me alive. It's in owning your own story that you embrace your unchangeable worth. In naming yourself the author of your own story, you can find your happy ending.

We can't change our pasts. But we can make peace with them — and we can change our futures by taking care of our inner selves, our souls, in the present.

We all have our own stories. We might not always choose the plot, but we can choose the theme. Let's make our stories about life, not just death. Let's make them about healing, not just pain. When we lose someone, the worst thing we can do is lose ourselves, too.

I'm empowered by uplifting and strengthening others' energy, which has led me to create a life all about inspiring others. My energy is about wisdom, light, and guidance. It's about influence, inspiration, and impact.

It's a gift born from years of sorrow and pain —but it has blessed me to pivot with purpose and use my story to help rewrite others'.

How will YOU write the next chapter of your story?

WENDY FAHEY: Wendy is a Spiritual Empowerment Coach, writer, and inspirational speaker. She's a common-sense straight shooter, whose knowledge comes from life experience, and researching until she can't see straight. She believes that cellular and spiritual alignment and living in the vibration of love is the cure for what ails humanity. She can be found at www.worldofwelllness.ca

> FREE FROM TRAUMA & FEAR

WHERE IS THE LOVE?

> *Feeling broken is a difficult cross to bear. Fixing that brokenness was equally difficult. I had to choose myself first - actively, every single day, discarding long held limiting beliefs, replacing them with empowering truths.*
>
> *~ Wendy Fahey*

As I listen to this song by the Payolas, the chorus jumps out at me, crying for attention. "Where is this love that will open the doors? Where is this love to make me cry out for more? Where is this love that comes from above? Where is this love?" How do you love yourself when mental illness has stolen everything from you, when trauma has replaced your ability to love yourself, when you can no longer live up to the ideals that society has set up for you, qualifying you as a productive human being? When you and those around you are judging you for your action or lack thereof? When your brain, your ego, and your trauma consistently tell you that you are not enough of anything? And most importantly, how do you love yourself when everything taught to you about love meant you had to sacrifice that love for Self and give it all to others?

Tough questions with equally tough answers. Merriam Webster defines love as "a feeling of strong or constant affection for a person." That definition felt a little lackluster. I looked up the definition of self-love next. It is defined as "an appreciation of one's own worth or virtue; proper regard for and attention to one's own happiness or well-being."

The person asking the questions in that paragraph is me, the person I used to be. I had no idea what self-love and self-care looked like. My home life as a child was extremely dysfunctional. My mother and father split when I was three. My father visited sporadically and became an absent father by the time I was seven. My mother met and married my stepfather. My mother, although kind-hearted and loving, was self-centered. Everyone's decisions somehow affected her, even when they weren't about her in the least. My stepfather was an egoic, abusive man, full of his own self-importance, a big man with an unhealed abused inner child. He did love my sister and me, however with my mother's permission and collaboration, he also terrorized us.

Fear creates negative feedback loops in the brain called trauma, and takes away the ability to respond, leaving only the ability to react. As an adult, I recognize my parents' trauma that created the circumstances of my childhood. As a child, I lived in a state of fear most of the time. I was bullied by students and teachers at school. The local library was my escape and the only safe space for my constantly jangled nerves.

Fast forward to adulthood, where the traumas of my childhood repeated themselves. I got married and had my first baby at 23, quickly followed by two more before the age of 27. My first husband was not much different from my parents. They say you marry who and what you know. By the age of 31, the marriage was over. I had terrible options when I was leaving this marriage. I chose to leave my children with their father. I needed to go to school because I needed a career to support myself and them. This was the one decision that would allow my children to have the most stable transition through our marriage imploding. It also turned out to be the best decision for them. It was not the best decision for me. I chose to become a victim of my circumstances.

When I left my children, I bankrupted myself on every level. I struggled with mental health issues through my marriage, which exacerbated when I left my children. I was diagnosed with multiple health issues over the years, including bipolar disorder. I had a string of bad relationships, further degrading my self-worth and mental health. I struggled with my

Where Is The Love?

weight, finding myself growing bigger and bigger, with no solution to lose it. Everything I tried didn't work. I had no idea how to love myself, and as a result, my children did not learn how to love themselves either.

I "met" my second husband in 2013. He was my ex-brother-in-law from my first marriage. His wife and my first husband are siblings. We were drawn to each other by the shared pain of being rejected by the same family. We began our relationship via this trauma bond; a terrible space to build a relationship foundation from. Once we moved in together, my mental health plummeted. I ballooned to 275 lbs. I couldn't work. I was the proverbial lump on the couch, unable to be the successful career woman I wanted to be. I was unable to function as a decent life partner. I was miserable. Something had to give.

On December 19, 2016, my husband was diagnosed with prostate cancer. We were given the diagnosis, handed a prescription and sent home. We didn't even have time to process the information because within 30 seconds of walking out of the doctor's office, his nephew called. He had been in a car accident, distracting us from the diagnosis. Christmas that year was filled with fear and dread. Neither of us knew how to process this information, and we had little support from the medical profession. When we asked the doctors if there was a way to eat that would support his healing, they said no. Doors to natural healing were being closed by the medical profession. I reached out to a good friend who works in natural health. She suggested the ketogenic diet. It was not yet mainstream in the diet world. I was intrigued, but I knew that I first needed to get my mindset right. I started to research, which included emotionally eating my way through bowls of ice cream, as well as bags of chips and dip, all while scrolling through keto groups on Facebook. I saw people my size losing enormous amounts of weight, and having amazing health issue reversals, including some of the health issues I was struggling with.

For the first time in a very long time, I had a glimmer of hope. My husband began his cancer journey listening to his doctors, starting with medication. It had terrible side effects, and I was losing him in a hormone disaster. This is what motivated me to start keto. It escaped me at the time that an external influence was necessary for me to get started.

I honestly wasn't sure if keto would work for me, however, I had a husband with cancer, and I was determined to reverse it holistically.

The one thing I knew for sure is that the body can heal itself, given the right conditions. Prophetic words indeed. I started in baby steps, eliminating sugar one week and losing six pounds. This gave me the first sparks of "Oh My God. This might work for me". Spurred on by that success, I then eliminated pasta, bread, and rice, loading up on veggies. More success! I was creating the correct conditions for my body, and it was responding positively. My husband needed to fly back home to Newfoundland because his mother passed away.

While he was gone, I went full keto. In the ten days he was gone, I dropped 12 lbs. and multiple inches. When he got home and saw me, the first thing he said was, "I want to do that!" Thankfully, he was at the end of his medication. He joined me in following keto. Keto caused his prostate serum antigen levels to drop like stone! His family doctor was impressed, however his urologist wanted him back on medication. My husband and I fought vehemently over whether he would go back on medication. I won that battle, and together, we went on to win the war, reversing his prostate cancer completely in ten months!

Through this journey, I started to learn what self-love meant. It meant healing the traumas of my childhood and adulthood. As I lost weight, many of the terrible things I experienced came out of my cells to be revisited. Healing your trauma, known as shadow work, is one of the deepest forms of self-love there is. It heals your body, your cells and most importantly, your mind. It begins regulating your nervous system, allowing you the ability to respond instead of reacting. Eating the right food for your body is a form of self-love. Being disciplined enough to stick with it is a form of self-care. I needed both in place to solidify the changes I was making. Self-love for me meant going out to buy clothes that fit properly on this newly emerging body. It meant feeling empowered when I wanted to cheat and didn't. It taught me that I cared more about the gains in self-love that I had made, rather than the food I was giving up. It meant learning that food is fuel; that going to the fridge to eat when you are bored is not self-love. It meant breaking habits that weren't serving me well, replacing them with ones that were in alignment

Where Is The Love?

with my goals and who I wanted to become. I lost 85 lbs. over the course of ten months. I reversed my bipolar completely, along with many of the other health issues I had.

To this day, doctors give me the side eye when I say I reversed my bipolar, and never hesitate to offer me medication. I stand my ground because I know that my mental health is the best it has ever been, regardless of their beliefs. Doctors are trained to mask symptoms, not seek the root cause. The root cause of my bipolar was unresolved trauma, food sensitivities, rampant victim mentality, nervous system dysregulation and gut health issues, creating a chemical shit storm in my brain. One of the most powerful days in my life was when I realized my brain was beginning to function properly for the first time in 35 years. I learned it is easier to ensure you are taking care of yourself through accountability. I spent time in keto groups, inspiring others, and sharing my knowledge, while soaking up their knowledge and support in return. When my husband's cancer disappeared and my brain was working, I became a keto social media influencer. I shared our story to inspire others to take control of their health, helping thousands of people make positive changes in their lives. Once the weight came off, I realized that I needed to up my self-care game another level. I added exercise to the mix because my body asked me to help it get stronger. I stayed accountable to myself by running a free exercise challenge on Facebook for the next two years. This helped me drop another five pounds, for a total loss of 90 lbs. I discovered Block Therapy; exercise, pain therapy and meditation in one. I liken it to shadow work for the body. This modality helped me release deeper trauma without having to cognitively work my way through it. It began releasing the pain that my body had been diligently carrying for over twenty years. It encouraged me to deepen my connection to this new body, to listen to what my cells were telling me. It kept my mental health stable, even on days when my brain refused to work. And, when my husband was diagnosed with prostate cancer again in January 2021, Block Therapy helped him reverse it over the course of several months. This modality is the ultimate self-love and self-care tool. I believe so deeply in its power, I became fully trained as a certified Block Therapist and Block Therapy Instructor. Each step I took, each trauma that healed, calmed my nervous system, and encouraged me to find new and better ways to love myself. As I grew and became more empowered, my son took notice. He moved back home for a while, wanting this transformation for himself.

This is the beautiful thing about healing. You not only heal yourself; you heal your ancestors and future generations. Your healing influences and encourages every person in your family to heal, whether they are aware of it or not. My son made the decision to pick up that healing torch. He has healed and together, we healed our fractured relationship. Healing myself poured over onto my sister's children, inspiring my oldest niece to begin the healing journey herself. I've proudly watched her doing the work, cheering her on from a distance. I learned how to set boundaries. Boundaries are the healthiest way to create love within yourself. I stopped allowing toxic people to stay in my life, creating space for people who were more in vibrational alignment with me. I learned to not be codependent. I got sober from a 20-year chronic cannabis addiction. I moved across the country to be closer to the mountains and nature. I even stopped colouring my hair because it wasn't in alignment with Who I Am. It's been an incredibly empowering journey. Has it been difficult? More difficult than you can imagine.

Feeling broken is a difficult cross to bear. Fixing that brokenness was equally difficult. I had to choose myself first - actively, every single day, discarding long held limiting beliefs, replacing them with empowering truths. I had to choose to love myself, to care for myself, to empower myself and others, every single day. It took longer to become second nature than I could have imagined. Some days, I wanted to give up.

There's a reason people don't volunteer for shadow work. It's the most challenging journey you will ever take. Looking deeply at yourself, taking personal responsibility for everything in your life, forgiving yourself and others for all the circumstances that contributed to who you became is painful, and can take you to dark places. Moving through the dark places brings you to a place of Light, Love, and Acceptance. To answer the question posed by the Payolas. "Where is this love?" It is inside you, hiding under layers of other people's ideas of who you are, buried under trauma and the terrible circumstances of your life. Don't

Where Is The Love?

be afraid to open that door. You will find the Love you seek within when you are brave enough to face the Truth. And when you find that love, you will discover the most important missing piece, that piece we all seek without knowing. Self-love is the pathway to loving yourself. It is the answer to all the questions asked above. It allows you to step into your Authentic Self.

Today, I am a Spiritual Empowerment Coach. I help people find their way back to themselves through cellular and spiritual alignment. I teach Block Therapy classes to align the cells and release trauma. I help my clients align spiritually through Kundalini Reiki and mindset coaching. Watching my clients heal the way I did motivates me to constantly improve myself, my skill set and my life, so I can be what I wish to see in the world. Authenticity comes through self-love. Embrace it!

Wendy Fahey

DEIDRE MIRAND: Deidre is an educator devoted to providing lessons in life and literature to today's youth. She has taught English Language Arts and writing for over 17 years. Encouraging young authors, she published a compilation of short stories titled, "Dream World" written by various students. Though Deidre has been a teacher and worked with children for over half of her life, she began questioning her purpose. On a road to self-discovery, she was diagnosed with MIT Family Translocation Renal Cell Carcinoma, a rare form of kidney cancer. This propelled her into finding her purpose in providing hope, help, and healing to those who doubt their God-given purpose on this earth. Her love for writing and mentoring encouraged her to launch her business as a Writing Coach, as she hopes to encourage future authors to get their stories out. Deidre is a Georgia girl with a Caribbean heart, a loving mother of one beautiful soul, a devoted daughter, a sister, and a mentor to many. She is a faithful follower of Christ and a true believer in the divinity of life. She is an educator and founder of Divine Destiny Consulting where she coaches future authors as well as editing projects.

> FREE FROM TRAUMA & FEAR

RELEASING FEAR

> *Letting go can be hard. When you deal with anxiety you can let a myriad of questions torment you. When we focus on what is right in front of us, the reality of the present moment, we tend to remain calm. I would soon see the benefit of this mindset shift.*
>
> *~ Deidre Mirand*

I used to think that cancer was my biggest fear; until I realized my fear turned into cancer.

I was in so much pain. My chest was hurting, I was heartbroken, emotionally exhausted, and alone. I was frustrated and spiraling out of control. The previous months had been the hardest of my life. It seemed like everything had come crashing down. Every relationship I had was being tested, my work was unfulfilling, and I was unable to control my empathy. Anxiety, insomnia, depression: you name it, I claimed it. I had hit rock bottom, but hadn't I been here before? Several times before, but this time felt different. I was ready for change. I had always questioned my why and I prayed earnestly for my purpose to be revealed. His answer came in the most unexpected manner.

As I walked through the dark valleys in the shadows of pain, heartbreak, and hurt, God walked with me. I began this journey, unaware of where it would lead me. I soon realized I had to take care of myself;

physically, mentally, and spiritually. Slowly, with guidance from my life coach, meditation, and practicing self-love, I began to heal. I began discovering, creating, learning to love myself, and nourishing my relationships. I was writing again, reflecting, rejuvenating, releasing, resting. I learned to let go. Letting go can be hard. When you deal with anxiety you can let a myriad of questions torment you. When we focus on what is right in front of us, the reality of the present moment, we tend to remain calm. I would soon see the benefit of this mindset shift.

I was healing emotionally, and spiritually. However, I began to experience some unfamiliar physical pain in my back, which led me to visit a chiropractor. He issued a body x-ray and determined I had two pinched nerves. Subsequently, the chiropractor urged me to take my x-ray to my primary doctor because he saw something unfavorable. How divine was it that this chiropractor spent 30 years as a radiologist and knew what he saw in my x-rays! I went to the doctor and shared my x-rays which revealed concern of a cancerous mass in my abdomen and pelvis. A CT Scan was needed to rule that out. When the results came back it revealed the mass was consistent with kidney cancer. I remember when I got the news, things went blank. Between hyperventilating, screaming, dragging myself on the floor, and vomiting, you would have thought I was a cartoon character! The one thing that I have always feared was cancer. This is when I gained a strength that I never knew I had. I put faith over fear and was transformed that day! I had to get a biopsy and eventually remove the mass on my kidney. There was a small pelvic lesion that could be where cancer had spread. A recommendation for an MRI and a visit with the oncologist were my next steps.

I now know God had been preparing me for this journey all along. As each day passed, I continued working on managing my emotions and communicating my needs. Surprisingly, what I had not experienced yet was fear. No matter what the doctors told me I knew my sickness will not end in death because healing is in heaven. No spirit of fear shall prosper.

The morning of my bone biopsy, I fretted about the pain. "My peace I leave with you, peace I give unto you, Deidre." All I had to do was just listen to God's word and obey. I began to cry and pant lying in the

Releasing Fear

frigid hospital bed, dreading the procedure. The nurse questioned my tears. "There's a mass on my kidney and I need this bone biopsy to be sure nothing is spreading." I sobbed. He assumed the diagnosis had me upset. I quickly cut him off, "I'm not upset about my diagnosis. It's the big needle you're about to put in my bone!" I was afraid of the pain that I hadn't even experienced, and God said, "My peace I give unto you." I relished that thought for a moment. Before I knew it, I was settled, but not soon enough. The nurse looked at me, "I'm going to give you a little something for anxiety." A chill pill. "I leave you with my peace." After receiving the calming Ativan and a brief discussion about the position I was to lay in… Nothing. I remember nothing. No pain! "My peace." I woke up in recovery! Did they even do the biopsy? "The peace I give is a gift the world cannot give." When He said it, I listened! The entire time, I was at peace.

It took about a week for the results to come in. When the biopsy results came in, I was ready! As soon as I got the notification, I told my sister and she began to cry. I said, "What are you crying for? Let's pray." Immediately I began, "Thank You, Lord. No matter what the results are I have peace, grace, and mercy on my side." Turns out there were rare, atypical cells on my bone that are not cancerous and need no further testing. Next came the partial nephrectomy, or kidney removal in layman's terms.

A few weeks later, I came out of surgery as He saw fit. Doctor Zurawin only had to remove the mass and part of the kidney! I remember God telling me I wouldn't be alone. As with my first procedure, I began ridiculously crying, agonizing about the anticipated pain. Jenne, my triage nurse, gazed at me and whispered, "Can I pray for you?" That's when I knew. I immediately settled. After a few pins and pricks, it was time for surgery. The lights were so bright, and the room was a sterile icebox. I felt the energy as soon as I was rolled into the operating room. The nurse to my right rubbed my arm gently. I was laying on the bed and the anesthesiologist, a heavyset black woman, leaned down as she asked for a napkin. She began to slowly wipe the tears from my eyes. She leaned in a little further and smoothly asked, "May I pray for you?" I was overwhelmed with God's mercy and protection. Of course, she could pray for me! The last thing I remember was hearing God's words as the entire medical team surrounded the bed. Was that common or am I truly blessed? The next thing I remember was my name being called and waking up that evening, Adonica, my twin sister, by my side. Again, He carried me and made sure I wasn't alone. I later found out the name of the nurses and anesthesiologist and I went to the hospital to hand-deliver them thank you cards. I needed them to understand their purpose on that day. My team of nurses, doctors, and anesthesiologists were all my angels.

A week later, the pathology report, disclosed that the type of cancer I had is called MIT Translocation Renal Cell Carcinoma. It's very rare and treated aggressively, however, no chemo or radiation treatment would be needed. I survived my greatest fear by letting it go.

The peace I experienced seems surreal, unearthly even. I felt closer to God than I had ever before. I have prayed over the years for many things; purpose, guidance, clarity. He answered my prayers. To many, it may seem odd that I find cancer to be an answer to my prayers! But why not? I haven't felt the need to ask God why me? Why cancer? It's because I know the answer is far too vast, uncomprehending, even to me. I am no longer depressed, haven't questioned God and I won't. Job from the Bible has been an inspiration because he was so strong, though he struggled physically and mentally. He had the "why me" syndrome. He questioned why he was still alive and why he survived his birth. He asked God why he couldn't have died after everything was taken from him. He was depressed. Why? It is a question that we always ask and there's nothing wrong with asking why. The thing is, God doesn't owe us an answer. He reminds us that though there is suffrage, we don't suffer alone. Job said, "God knows the way that I take. And when he has tested me, I shall come forth as gold! Though he slayed me I still trust." I can't help but see all the blessings right in front of me. I feel proud that God has chosen me. My tender heart has strengthened, my confused mind is clearer, my wavering spiritual walk is relentless, and I have an appreciation for my family that I haven't had in a while. Look at how God lined everything up for me, his baby. He tested every relationship in my life. I was going through so much to discover myself before the diagnosis. I

Releasing Fear

was in the process of learning to love me, the one He created. Zion, my son, moved in with his father, I got FMLA approved, and the space I needed from my previous relationship. The pain in my back led me to a chiropractor, who sent me to the doctor and the ball got rolling. But God! Though I had a natural, human, bonafide tantrum, I settled very quickly in the fact that God makes no mistakes. This was his plan and there isn't much we as humans can do about things when God has a plan! During a later conversation, Adonica stated, "We've been thinking Deidre is the weak one all this time, but she might just be the strong one." I knew that's what they were thinking about me my whole life. But I am not weak! I am very strong! God has been working me out! If they only knew. "Greater is he that is in Me than he that is in the world." That's a scripture somewhere in the Bible. Mom said this morning that is through me and my connection to God that she sees life differently. That meant more to me than she will know because Mom has always been the super Christian to me.

Though I am a Christian, I had let go of religion and tradition. I will always follow Christ because He is my savior, literally! But I had to let go of the judgments and expectations from religion and tradition. I desire to be so spiritually connected to Him that others see the God in me. No pride, just love. I want them to see my peace, and my strength and know that I only attribute it to God. I want to be a beacon of light for Him! I want to be a billboard of his grace and mercy. I want to focus on life, and good memories, so my son can see a better me. I want to embrace His plans. But there were times in my life when I allowed sin to convince me that God would judge me and punish me, not eternally, but here on Earth. I trusted myself instead of trusting God. He makes no mistakes and once I realized that, my world changed. So, I embraced it. Praying and repenting and asking forgiveness daily. I will continue to grow in God and connect with Him regardless of what the world tells me! I want to learn more about His goodness, and know more of His word, so when I do go to heaven He can say, "Well done."

I sat down to talk with my sister about the joy of my journey thus far. Adonica said, "It's not what God is doing to you, it's what he is doing through you!" I love being his servant. Galatians 5:22 - 23 says, "but the fruit of the spirit is love, joy, peace forbearance, kindness, goodness, faithfulness, gentleness, and self-control. I say to myself, Deidre in all that you do, bear the fruit of the spirit always!

That anxiety I claimed for over 20 years is now liberated. I let go of worry because it came from fear and you can't worry and trust God at the same time. There are many causes of fear. Some are learned fears, and some are birthed from ignorance. Some rise out of imagination, like the narratives I have created in my head to justify my feelings. Ultimately, all fears are choices that we make with doubt being the root cause. I had a poor self-image, no confidence, and beat myself up. Too often was I defeated before I began. My fear caused anxiety, afflicting my whole life. I dealt with guilt in which I allowed my past failures to gain control of my present life. Many things can happen as a result of living in fear. It crippled my capacity to think clearly and make good decisions, always worrying about whether or not I'm making the right decision. It has also damaged my relationships with people, especially those I'm closest to because I was afraid to love and trust. My relationship with God had been most challenged by my fear. I have since learned that God gave us grace and He won't attack me. My relationship with Him won't flourish in fear because He is forgiving.

During a morning meditation whilst recovering from my surgery, I chose to focus on my future and recognize my fears. I was transcendently calm as a purplish turquoise light radiated from the space in the center of my eyes. I asked my future self what she wanted, and the following words resonated. "Peace, nature, water, write and you're alone, but not alone, you're by yourself and at peace with that." I also repeatedly heard, "failure." The word fear had been so prevalent in the last year, and it controlled my life. I realize I'm afraid of failure, not doing what God intended me to do. In every aspect of my life, I'm afraid of taking steps toward anything because I don't know if it's part of the path that was created for me. I've been fighting myself my whole life, not doing things I want to do out of fear. God constantly shows me to not be afraid. I heard myself say, "No more!" It was at that moment that I knew my purpose. I want to take chances. If it doesn't work out it is not failure, it's learning. He made me an educator, a teacher, a learner. So, I stopped preventing

Releasing Fear

myself from learning and started living my best life. I am meant to learn about this new form of cancer I had. I know what to do with my future. I am going to live it! I am meant to educate, but the classroom was just the beginning. I was made on purpose for a purpose. My time is now. Like a butterfly I will evolve, I am evolving, my energy redirected. I'm blessed.

There had been a course of miracles going on in my life. At one point I was so low, there was nowhere else to go, nothing else to see, until I saw Him… within me.

Deidre Mirand

MILA FINLEY: Mila, The Intuitive Wordsmith, writes personalized poems and stories in order to heal and guide those in hardship. She wrote the children's story "Bonnie's Best Birthday" and has many others she plans to publish in order to nourish children's minds with creativity, and love, as well as to allow them to grow without fear and limitations. Mila is passionate about helping sensitive empathic people experiencing anything in the realm of fear (anxiety, panic, PTSD, etc.) to overcome their limitations, so they can follow their dreams, manifest their desires, and fulfill their purpose. She has created a course to help navigate the subconscious mind out of fear and into love, involving all the steps she took to overcome decades' worth of panic attacks and trauma. If you'd like to see all that she has available and/or for a community of support and love, follow Mila on Facebook at: The Intuitive Wordsmith.

FREE FROM TRAUMA & FEAR

FROM LIVING AND FEARING DEATH TO LIVING AND LOVING LIFE

> *Finding who I am as my own beautiful soul helped me realize that I've always been good enough, pretty enough, and worthy. It was never who I pretended to be or what I looked like on the outside that defined me. It's who I am and the light I shine from the inside that defines me.*
>
> *- Mila Finley*

Growing up if you would have asked me, "How do you feel?" my answer would have always been, "Alone." I wasn't always alone, I saw family, schoolmates, strangers, and friends at times… But inside I always felt alone. I felt like no one understood me, that no one liked me, and that everyone was judging me.

From a young age I suffered from panic attacks. They consumed my life for a long time. I didn't feel safe anywhere, I would randomly feel intense sensations inside my body telling me I needed to run and get help, that I was dying. No one could understand how miserable these feelings were. Nobody knew how to help me.

Growing up I didn't think my own parents liked me. "How could anyone like me, I'm a burden on everyone." I thought they were disappointed in how 'broken' I was, so I'd strive to be "perfect" to prove my worth. I'd do anything and be anyone to prove I was good enough, but I felt like they didn't notice.

I had to parent my sister at a young age, and I put a lot of pressure on myself to be a Mom figure. This mixed with me trying to be "perfect" for my parents led to a lot of self-abuse. I'd be hard on myself for not being smarter, prettier, skinnier, and whatever other people considered to be "good enough."

Through trying to be all of these things I wasn't being Me. This detachment from my soul caused a lot of anger, hate, rebellion, depression, and overall lack of care about myself. Many times, I wanted to run away or disappear. Then I would hate myself for feeling all of these things because I was being "Bad."

I didn't feel safe expressing myself. I felt like a lion trapped in a small cage being surrounded by the random bouts of anger, coping with drugs and alcohol, and the blame that fell on my shoulders. When I did express my anger my parents either completely ignored me, yelled or used my outbursts against me; saying I am a bad kid, an adolescent, or telling me that they'd call the cops and send me to DH (kids jail). I got so sick from the stress.

I carried this detached, miserable version of myself through three relationships that mirrored exactly how I felt about myself. I went into them innocent and vulnerable, hoping that someone could love me and fill the emptiness I felt inside.

I got my first "real" boyfriend when I was a freshman in high school. He was my first kiss at the age of 15. I liked him because he was really nice to me and funny. Turns out he also had problems of his own. He hurt himself in front of me, threatened to kill himself if I broke up with him and ended up cutting himself with a knife on the bus right next to me. During the months that this went on I was already dealing with working, trying to care for my sister, and worrying about my mom. I feared that my ex would come to my work and shoot me, I had dreams that he chased me with a knife. He was so angry I wasn't sure what he was capable of.

My next relationship was with a man older than me. I was 17 and he was 25. I met him online, and he asked me to be his girlfriend after

From Living And Fearing Death To Living And Loving Life

a month. I had nothing to lose so I said, "yes." He was from Australia, so I thought he'd be different from the immature boys that I went to school with, or the American men that abused my mom. He happened to be in the US that month and wanted to meet me. He was controlling from the start but he acted like it was playful, I felt the red flags but kept going to try and understand him better. He was mentally, physically, and emotionally abusive. He flicked me in my ear when I said something he didn't like such as calling him silly. He'd slap, punch, and bang my face on the ground. He'd call me fat and say he needed an 'upgrade'.

Much of this was after I left to go to Australia with him. I was in a foreign country with him for four months. Why would I go to another country with him? I didn't want the life I had, I felt I had nothing to lose.

Looking back, I see he didn't treat me any worse than I treated myself. He cheated constantly, mostly chatting with many, many girls online, calling them his girlfriend, saying the same things to them that he did to me.

"Does 'I love you' mean anything to anyone anymore?" I asked myself. Being the empathic person I've always been, I knew he was just very insecure and felt he needed validation, so I tried to give him even more of me, until there was nothing left. No matter what I did he wouldn't stop talking to other girls, he wouldn't stop hitting me or blaming me for everything. I cried all the time, my heart felt broken, and he'd laugh. The airport was the last time he got to see me cry.

When I got back to my mom's house, I got an app to find friends. I was sick of guys but I met a guy in my area and we went out as friends. After that day I rarely left his house. He became my boyfriend a little while later. I was in a very vulnerable state, so I basically just molded in order to fit his lifestyle. He was a weed dealer and although I've never used drugs or alcohol. I didn't mind that he did. He was also addicted to playing computer games. That's what he did day in and day out.

I really liked his personality. He was kind of controlling but I could tell he had a sensitive heart behind the tough wall he built. My breaking point in this relationship was when an ex-roommate broke into the house and then tried to break in two more times. The first time I came home alone and felt something was off, then I saw the broken window and didn't know if he was still in there waiting for me.

I freaked out.

I didn't want to be there, but my ex said if I couldn't stay inside, hold a gun and protect the house then I was "weak" and not good enough for him. Wanting to prove myself as "good enough" for him I sat on the couch paralyzed with fear. After a week I dropped into a massive panic attack and my mom came to pick me up. It wasn't until I was in the hospital for three days with acute renal failure and he didn't come to see me that I finally started realizing that he only really cared about himself and that me and my mom were misunderstanding each other.

It was hard to let him go, but I'm glad I did. I could've never had the growth, connection, and understanding of my soul or my family that I have now if I would've stayed in any of those relationships.

This detachment I had from my soul caused me to feel the need for validation from everyone but especially from my boyfriends and family. I felt the need for a lot of attention and I felt discontentment when I was alone.

All of this caused a lot of codependency.

I relied on others to tell me if I was good enough, worthy, and pretty or not. I'd try to go out with people or just numb my brain with TV to avoid my feelings and traumas.

Throughout these years I feared everything and had too many panic attacks to count. I wore all neutral colors not wanting to be seen, fearing what everyone outside of me was thinking about me.

Turns out my value and the love for Me was inside my soul the whole time.

Finding who I am as my own beautiful soul helped me realize that I've always been good enough, pretty enough, and worthy. It was never who I pretended to be or what I looked like on the outside that defined me. It's who I am and the light I shine from the inside that defines me.

This isn't just me. Everyone is good enough, pretty enough, and worthy. It's an amazing opportunity to be different, we can offer the world a new perspective.

From Living And Fearing Death To Living And Loving Life

My exes didn't treat me the way they did because they were bad or I wasn't good enough, it was because I attracted like-minded souls, other people who (like me) didn't like or know themselves. People who projected their insecurities onto me without realizing or without the knowledge of how to change.

That being said, once I saw my worth, I realized I should have never let anyone treat me that way. I should've left and allowed them the time and space to heal. No one can heal you, but yourself. My sticking around was enabling them to act out of habit and subconscious. I told myself I was sticking around to help them but really I stayed out of fear-- fear of losing them to someone else and thus proving my unworthiness, the fear of being alone, and the fear that no one else would want my broken self.

Now I know this simply isn't true.

Over time I learned that my parents are amazing souls that just carried a lot of hurt. I'm so thankful to be closer to them now. I understand they were both very busy working, dating, and trying to get through life like all of us. If it weren't for them, I wouldn't be here. I wouldn't have experienced the "bad" in order to appreciate and love the "good" life has to offer. I also would not have learned from the hurdles and lessons that they experienced.

Forgiving and loving everyone in my past and present has had an amazing impact on my healing, and on my relationships with not only others, but especially with myself.

During the PTSD from the break-ins, I tried medication. It took the symptoms down slightly, but it was just a Band-Aid. I realized I needed to get to the root cause if I was ever going to heal, and so it began...

My healing journey took me through energy healing, inner child work, manifestation, and much more. Looking back, all of the events in my life were a blessing. I chose a rocky road, but it gave me a shove into healing.

I got to the point where I couldn't stop thinking that I was dying, I wasn't alive, I was living death.

I had the choice to die with no purpose or legend or to change everything about my life and find a better way to live. Once I made that

Hearttalks

decision God presented me with courses, books, oracle cards, mentors, etc. to learn how to heal my chronic stress and "incurable mental illness."

I no longer have panic attacks these days, I've learned what relaxation feels like and I know what to do when anxiety comes up. Now my purpose is to help others with "incurable" anxiety, panic, childhood trauma, etc. to get out of that hopeless hole and to get into the light of abundance, joy, and love.

If you resonate with my story at all and if you want to begin your healing journey but unsure of how, here are three things you can do right now to get started:

1. Write five things you're grateful for and five things you love about yourself every day for 30 days. It may be difficult at first, but it will get easier. I promise.
2. Acknowledge that all your relationships are mirroring patterns within yourself. When someone does something you don't like, journal it. Then underneath write how that relates to how you feel and what you don't like about yourself.
3. Find a mentor who knows personally what you're going through, someone you resonate with and commit to your self-healing. We are not meant to do this alone.

The journey isn't always easy, but it's so worth it!

Mila Finley

STEPHANIE ASHTON: Stephanie lives a fulfilling life in Sarasota, Florida with her husband and two dogs. Stephanie regularly speaks to groups about not quitting on yourself. She's been a mental health warrior her whole life and a chronic illness warrior for 23 years. Her friends lovingly nicknamed her "Sassy" for her perspective on life.

LOVE & HEALING

A LETTER TO 18-YEAR-OLD ME: A LITTLE LIFE ADVICE

> *Stop caring so much about what others think. You'll never be able to please everyone so stop living for the approval of others and live for yourself.*
>
> *~ Stephanie Ashton*

Hello Gorgeous,

I've been doing some thinking lately as I recently turned 40 and I've been thinking of you. I'm not sure if you've ever wanted advice from your older self. Even if you didn't, here are some tidbits that I'd like to share with you. I'm not holding back; I'm going to be honest with you about everything.

First things first: you're going to make it through - through this and through everything. At 18 years old I know that you're dying to be a "real" adult, with a real job, a real paycheck, your own space, your own responsibilities, and no one to tell you what to do. Please slow down. Take five minutes and take a deep breath. Trust me when I say that the vast majority of being a "real" adult consists of the never-ending chores of laundry, doing the dishes, and trying to decide what to have for dinner. It's rather boring. Slow down and enjoy the present moment. Soak it all in. Adulthood can wait. Taking baby steps towards independence will be exciting but take mental notes, or better yet, journal. There's going to be so much that you will forget. You're going to want to look back and see your journey with all of your amazing growth. I know that things have been tough lately and you're feeling overwhelmed. You've been trying to carry the weight of the world on your shoulders for too long now. Life has already thrown some ugly experiences at you, hasn't it? Don't let the pain harden your heart. Put it to good use.

Share your story and your truth. It will help people to feel less alone in life. Doing this gives your pain, your life story, a purpose. Believe it or not, sharing your story later turns into a non-profit that has helped many. It will become a passion project of yours. It's okay to be scared. The world can be chaotic, cold, and cruel. Don't let that stop you. Be brave my dear and stop letting fear hold you back. Feel the fear and then do it anyway. That's courage. I know that the bullies have you convinced that you are fat and unattractive. You're not. You are a gorgeous young girl with a beautiful figure. There will come a day where you will look at yourself at this age and wonder how you ever thought that THIS was fat. It takes time to unravel your body image issues and I wish that you learned to love and cherish your body sooner, but you do eventually learn that you are not your body size, and that body size does not determine your worth. Forget about those bullies. I know that they played a major role in your childhood, but they don't matter. You will prove them wrong so don't doubt yourself-- not for one second. You have a bright path ahead.

Be gentle with yourself. You're going to make mistakes. Lots of them. It's okay. That's how we learn. Pick yourself up when you fall and dust yourself off. Failure is a part of life, not the end of the world. Failing at something does not mean that you yourself are a failure. It means that there's room for you to grow and more for you to learn. Find the lesson in the experience and then keep moving forward. You will think that you are not good enough, but I promise--you are. You are so much more than enough. You will always be more than enough. Stop looking outside yourself for your worth. Cut yourself some slack. Despite what you think, you do not have to be perfect. Perfection is nothing more than an illusion. Salvador Dali once said, "Have no fear of perfection.

A Letter to 18-Year-Old Me: A Little Life Advice

You'll never reach it." I agree with him. It's an ideal, something that can be worth striving for, but it is not the be all or end all of life. There will always be room to grow. Walk away from people and things that no longer serve you. It's not selfish. Sometimes we outgrow stuff. Stand up for yourself. Set healthy boundaries and hold them. It might feel uncomfortable in the moment but hold fast, you can do it! Standing up for yourself pays off in the long run. You are worthy of being put first.

Ask for help! There is no shame in needing assistance. In fact, asking for help shows immense strength. It's ok to sleep with stuffed animals and soft, fluffy blankets. You'll do it for the rest of your life. If people tease you about it, let them. They obviously don't know how awesome it feels to create a nest of soft blankets and stuffies and curl up with a good book. It's okay to name said stuffed animals. I still do. Right now, I have two unicorn stuffies named Faith and Hope. That way, no matter what is going on, I will always have faith and hope. Be yourself. Be unapologetically you. Don't edit yourself trying to make other people comfortable. Do not let those who are afraid of your light dim it. You see things differently and do things differently and that, coupled with your deep sense of compassion, will make the world a better place. Embrace your weird. It's part of what makes you who you are. You're unique and one of a kind. Celebrate that uniqueness and the uniqueness of others. Allow yourself to be vulnerable. I know that it's scary and it opens yourself up to being hurt. However, it's what opens yourself up to being loved. Take a deep breath and risk it. It's worth it. Laugh. A lot. Do it every day, multiple times a day. Laughter truly is the best medicine. Oh, and your laugh is not annoying, it's unique and genuine. Don't hold it back. Your sense of humor and ability to laugh at life, especially your ability to laugh about the dark stuff, draws people to you in a good and uplifting way. Don't get caught up in taking life and yourself so seriously. Have fun with life!

Stop caring so much about what others think. You'll never be able to please everyone so stop living for the approval of others and live for yourself. Accept that there will be people who won't/don't like you. It's not the end of the world. Let's be honest, you don't even like everyone, so why worry about them! You'll find your tribe and be surrounded by the people who appreciate you for you. If you're ever in your head about this put on "The Middle" by Jimmy Eat World. Turn the volume up. Loud. Louder. Sing it at the top of your lungs, loud and proud while throwing yourself an impromptu 30 second dance party. It will absolutely make you feel better. Embrace the lyrics "It's only in your head you feel left out or looked down on . . . Live right now, yeah, just be yourself. It doesn't matter if it's good enough for someone else." This song is one of your anthems. Don't quit on yourself. I know that you frequently have suicidal thoughts. Please don't act on them. I know that it's scary but please speak up and tell a friend or loved one what's on your heart. There's no shame in having these thoughts. Honestly, I still have them, but they've slowed down in frequency, and I know that they're just thoughts. You don't need to act on them, but you do need to talk about them. Sharing what you're going through with a trusted person will lesson your burden and make it easier to power through the tough times. The tough times don't last. You do. I know that sometimes it's difficult to know who's voice you're hearing in your head. A lot of what you think is your voice is the voices of others, like your parents and your teachers. It can get confusing. Please take some time to sit and figure out which voice is yours. Then listen to yourself. Keep listening to your true, authentic voice. Own your life and make decisions that you feel good about, not what you think other people are expecting of you. Pay more attention to your studies. Take the time to learn how to effectively take notes and study. It might be annoying and dull, but you'll regret not putting in more effort. Finish your degree. You'll have your reasons for walking away from college, but they aren't good ones. I'm going to be honest – this is a time when drugs and alcohol play a prominent role in your life. I'm not going to tell you to "just say no" like they taught you in the D.A.R.E. program. That's quite laughable in my opinion because I know from experience that it's a lot easier said than done. My dear girl, I know why you're doing this but despite what you think, drugs and alcohol are not the solution to managing or suppressing your feelings and memories. This is not the way to deal or heal from the trauma you endured as a young girl. Only dealing with your emotions can do that. Take the help to walk away from that life the first time it is offered. Accept the help but don't let yourself be defined by the labels they try to put on

A Letter to 18-Year-Old Me: A Little Life Advice

you. I wasted a lot of time being attached to labels that didn't serve me. Breathe and dig deep in therapy. The coping skills and support you get while processing trauma will be life changing for you. You'll discover and nourish your inner strength. You're going to run into users and abusers, people who will take advantage of your kindness and generosity. Be kind and generous anyway. Don't let them harden your heart.

Create a daily gratitude practice for yourself. Write five different things that you are grateful for each day. Make a journal specifically for this. It might seem trite some days but keep plugging away at it. Having a gratitude practice will carry you through the tough times and it will help you celebrate and remember the good ones.

I know that some of the adults in your life have let you down. I know that it will be challenging but please try to be forgiving. You don't need to forget, and you don't need to keep them in your life; you do need to find a path to forgiveness. This is for your mental and emotional health; it has nothing to do with them. Try to remember that they too are human and like you they make mistakes. Be kind with your inner child. She's hurting and needs your love. Be gentle with her.

It's never too late to be the person you needed when you were younger. There are many wishes and promises you made to yourself along the way that have yet to be fulfilled. There are places you've been dreaming of visiting your whole life. I will absolutely do my best to make those past promises come true. I promise that I will take all the advice I have given you for myself. How can I expect you to take it if I don't model it?

Today you look quite different than you do at 18, both inside and out. You probably didn't expect to turn out this way; I think you would be surprised at the person you've become. You will be quite proud and thrilled with the way you've turned out. Keep being unapologetically you.

Love,
Yours Truly,

Stephanie Ashton

TRACEY LIPP: Tracey is a Registered Master of Social Work. Her private practice includes Equine Assisted Psychotherapy and trauma therapy with adults, adolescents, and children. Tracey also partners with Tricia Rudy and Lindsay Hachey at Harmony with Horses. Tracey strives to live a life true to herself. For her this means being present, mindful, authentic, honest and of service to others, while paying attention to her own need for self-compassion. The road is often a bumpy one. But, with the help of her own horse healers, she is moving closer to wholeness. Tracey is aware of the importance and power of connection, both to ourselves, to nature and to all beings and looks for opportunities to nurture connections whenever possible.

LOVE & HEALING

TINKER

> *I don't need to be someone I'm not. I am worthy of love just because I am. I no longer need the approval of others just to be.*
>
> *~ Tracey Lipp*

I was eight months old before I met him, my dad. Little did I know that my not knowing him for the first eight months of my life would set the stage for the remainder of our relationship on this earth. The dance that best describes our relationship was of me chasing him and doing everything that I could think of for him to pay attention to me, to give me even a morsel of his time and affection.

Usually, the attention that I got was more negative than positive which meant I just had to try harder. The message that I took from this back and forth was that I just hadn't learned the right steps to the dance. I still had to work harder to not step on his toes.

What I didn't know then but seems clear to me now is that my dad didn't really know himself. He was fighting his own inner demons and he cared for us the best way he knew based on a complicated story of his own. What little he shared with me as he got older was that his own father was abusive and violent. He described his mother as loving, kind, and caring. According to my father, when he was 15 years old, he and his older brother kicked their father out of their house to protect their mother and siblings. My father never spoke about his father and whenever I would ask, as I grew older, he would say he didn't know anything about him. This was clearly an area of his life that he preferred to keep cloistered away, under lock and key and buried deep inside his broken heart.

I also didn't know that as a little girl but can now understand that he was bleeding out the anger and sadness that he was trying so hard to keep covered over. My dad was in the Royal British Navy and was overseas, in Asia, at the time of my birth. My birth story was quite simple but as it was told to me over the years, it set the stage for not only how I perceived myself but how I believed my dad perceived me as well.

I was born in a little naval base in Wroughton, England. Although the "o" sound is long just like oatmeal, the running joke became that I was born in Wroughton, pronounced rotten. I became referred to as the rotten kid. I am sure when it started, the story was meant in fun. But, to a little girl, that message stuck with me throughout my childhood, even though I had no idea of its significance. Nothing like being considered the rotten kid to boost your self-esteem, right? I was also told that I was in a hurry to be born and my mother didn't even make it to the delivery room before I made my appearance. This message also became one of me being impatient, in a hurry, impulsive and impetuous.

I don't actually remember the time when my father began referring to me as a Tinker. I might have been quite young, but my first recollection of it would have been when I was around 10 or 11 years old. My dad referred to me as a Tinker when he was frustrated with me. I didn't know what the term Tinker meant at the time, but I knew that it wasn't a term of endearment. What I have since come to learn is that a Tinker, as he used it, meant that I was mischievous. The term Tinker was another label that my dad put on me that supported my belief that I didn't please him. I also didn't realize just how important the term Tinker would be for my healing later in life.

The year I turned 12 was a pivotal year. Like many kids who believe themselves to be rotten, mischievous, impetuous, and hard to love, I started to hang out with a crowd that were not really doing anything

Tinker

bad, they were just a bit rebellious. One day we were loitering in the stairwell of an apartment building in our neighborhood. We weren't doing anything particularly shocking, but someone must have been upset by our presence and called the police. I was put in the back of the police cruiser and taken home. My parents were both home at the time and I remember being absolutely terrified of what would happen when I got there. The police explained to my parents why they had brought me home and that they would leave the matter to them. I remember the officer telling my mother that I was a good kid, but probably just hanging out with the wrong crowd. My mom was terribly upset and told me to go to my room. My dad didn't say a thing and just left the room. I did as my mom told me and closed my bedroom door. Hoping that by shutting myself in I would have some time to catch my breath and give my parents time to calm down too. A couple of minutes later my dad opened my bedroom door with a belt in his hand. He didn't speak, he didn't even look at me. I just noticed that his eyes were vacant, and he lost control. He started whipping me with his belt and the thought that I might die became real. I begged and pleaded for him to stop and it was like he wasn't even present and couldn't hear me. My mom came flying into my room and grabbed his arm to make him stop. It took her several tries and lots of pleading, but he finally stormed out of the room while I sat curled up in a ball in the corner of my bed. I have never been more afraid for my life or more afraid of my dad. My dad never apologized for hurting me or for losing control and we never spoke of what happened that day again. It just became etched in my memory and the imprint for my stress response every time I faced someone who seemed to have lost control. I would freeze and then try to figure out what I could do to please them. I learned to stay ahead of my dad's disfavour by anticipating his mood, paying attention to his body language and his tone of voice. I knew that he needed time to unwind when he got home from work and it was best to give him time, space and breathing room or suffer the consequences of his agitation and impatience. I learned that if I needed anything to ask my mom. She knew how to soften the blow with him most of the time. She understood him and managed him well. This became our new dance.

Hearttalks

I have always been a horse lover. I was one of those little girls who dreamed of having her own horse and asked for a pony every birthday or Christmas. I would spend hours reading horse books and drawing pictures of horses. My mother finally agreed to let me have riding lessons when I was about 13. At that point I could help pay for it with my babysitting money. The magical fantasy I had about horses paled in comparison to the reality of the connection I felt when I was finally in their presence. This longing remained constant over the years, even though horses would come in and out of my life. I consider myself a bit of an expert when it comes to grief. Sure, I have some formal education and training but my real expertise came because of real life experience. I would describe my experience of grief, as Robert Kastenbaum labels it, bereavement overload. There have been several times during my almost 58 years that I thought I had reached my bottom.

My first significant loss occurred at the end of my first marriage. Although it was the right decision for us at that time, the pain I felt was something deeper than I had ever experienced before. The year following our separation I became ill and aware of anxiety that I believe had always been present, but I had been managing. I began experiencing panic attacks that were so scary and debilitating I thought I was going to die. I knew that I would not be able to manage on my own anymore, so began counselling and taking medication. There was a period of time when I felt so disconnected from myself and my ability to cope that I thought about ending my life. But, somehow the will to keep trying and the love for my children kept me going.

My second major loss came in 2000 when my mother, who was my best friend, my protector, my safe place became ill and died. My world was absolutely shattered, and I honestly didn't know how to move on without her. But, at that time, my dad was an absolute puddle and I thought it was my duty to take care of him. So, I did what I thought I needed to do and bury my own overwhelming sadness away to tend to him.

There was a period not long after my mother died that my dad was questioning his own will to live. My brothers and I supported him the best way that we could, and he was able to turn the corner to the possibility of going on without her. About a month after our mom died, my dad announced to me that a friend of his from work was going to be moving into their home because she needed a place to stay. As you can imagine, this was an absolute shock to me. This is a whole other story for another time but is significant in my journey of complicated grief. It was at that time that I switched from feeling the need to protect my father to the need to protect my mother, her memory and her legacy. I became stuck in my grief while my dad became consumed with his new life.

My third significant loss came two years later when our oldest brother, Cameron, died suddenly of a heart attack. Cameron was my hero and the father figure I had always looked up to. The two most important people in my life were now gone and I felt so alone in this world. I still don't know how I was able to get out of bed in the morning, but somehow, I put on a brave face and managed to face the day. After my father's "friend" moved into my mom's house and up until Cameron died, I hadn't spoken with my dad. It was just too painful. But, when Cameron died, we needed to go to British Columbia to be with his family and support them the best way we could. So, this began our journey back together. Cameron's death also made me realize that not speaking with my dad also meant that my children would grow up not knowing him and I couldn't do that to them. I had come to be fairly good at wearing the brave faced mask and put other people's feelings and needs ahead of my own.

My dad and I re-established our dance and slipped back into our way of being with each other. This dysfunctional dance would continue between us until he died on July 1, 2019.

When my dad became terminally ill with Chronic Obstructive Pulmonary Disease in 2017, I became aware of an emotional shift and my longing for the connection of horses became so strong that I just had to listen to my heart. I realized that the best healing for me was when I was with horses. So, I started riding again and made sure that horses were a constant. My heart was finally feeling a bit lighter and the nurturing connection I needed was available to me through my horse healers.

I thought I had hit bottom in my earlier experiences of loss, but it was actually after my dad died that the bottom finally fell out. All of the years of loss and pain that had been stuffed away came crashing to the surface. It was no longer necessary for me to pretend I was okay for anyone and I could finally begin to feel all of it. I was finally able to allow my heart to heal from the death of my mother and brother. I no longer needed to protect them.

My pain culminated in emotional paralysis for a little while until I met Mystic. Mystic is the most beautiful black and white Gypsy Vanner Percheron. She appeared in my life just when I needed her the most. My heart had been searching for a place to belong where I could offer Equine Facilitated Psychotherapy.

Just as had often happened throughout my life, when I release my heart's intention to the universe, the universe answers. I was given the opportunity to meet with the team at Harmony with Horses to discuss the possibility of collaborating. Little did I know that that first meeting would be the beginning of my heart becoming unburdened and releasing the chains that I had worked so hard to keep locked.

I had come to believe, through a series of synchronistic experiences, that I was destined to have a black and white draft horse in my life. I had thought it would be a black and white Clydesdale, but I have also come to know that what we think we need and what actually shows up for us are not always the same thing. I was absolutely awestruck when I laid eyes on Mystic. When I walked into the field to meet her and her herd mates, something magical happened.

As I came to learn afterwards, Mystic is characterized as gregarious, mischievous, lacking in boundaries, and unaware of her size and strength. She is also known to be gentle, sweet, and loving. Mystic came to stand in front of me and gently press her massive head onto my chest. She then proceeded to walk along one side of me, around behind me and come to stand on the other side tucked up against me. She then took her long neck and gently wrapped it around me as if protecting me in a warm embrace. She held this position for a couple of minutes while my heart was bursting with love. She then proceeded to repeat this whole sequence a second time ending again in wrapping her neck around me in a safe, comforting, and protective hug. We were all speechless at her offering of love and connection. Knowing that by putting

Tinker

herself in this position she was so vulnerable. I was still processing the beauty and emotional significance of my introduction to Mystic when we met for the second time. I was meeting with the Harmony with Horses team and participating in a couple of Facilitated Equine Experiential Learning (FEEL) activities. When asked which horse I would like to have accompany me as part of the process, I of course, chose Mystic. She was excited, curious, and fully engaged in the activity with me. We were both invited to choose a card from Linda Kohanov's Way of the Horse: Equine Archetypes for Self-Discovery deck. To say that the cards we both chose were exactly what we need would be an understatement.

My message in that moment was that it was time to release, let go, and embrace all of the parts of myself that I had for so many years kept locked away in my heart. That all of the parts of me are welcome and worthy of being seen, loved, and nurtured.

We all have darkness and light inside of us and both belong. I had come to a place of acknowledging that the darkness inside of me was the me that was too much, too busy, too loud, and too talkative. The parts of me that my dad couldn't handle and didn't know what to do with. I think the part of me that reminded him of himself.

The light inside of me was where my tenderness and need for nurturing lived. The part that had been neglected all these years not by anyone other than me. But, like Mystic, the black and white blended beautifully together. We were wrapping up our session when I asked Mystic if she would like to be groomed for a few minutes. This is when the lightning struck to solidify my forever connection with her. I went to look for her grooming bucket but was told that it wasn't marked Mystic. She had come to Harmony with Horses known by another name.

Her previous name had been Tinker. I wish I could properly describe what I felt in that moment. It was a combination of euphoria, nausea, joy, and disbelief. You just can't make this stuff up. It was perfectly clear to me that this magnificent being had come into my life at just the right time to help me finally heal.

Mystic is teaching me that I don't need to be someone I'm not. I am worthy of love just because I am. I no longer need the approval of others just to be.

Hearttalks

The way I see myself within my family has shifted and I am much more comfortable in the role of supporter than leader. I have given up the need to prove my worth and I am ready to tell my story from a place of honesty. Healing is a lifelong journey, but a journey worth taking. I recently read a quote by Nicholas Goodman that captures where I am at beautifully. Mr. Goodman writes, "She was a heavenly tapestry, blending threads of night and day into shades of dawn. It was the intertwining of light and darkness that made her a masterpiece". Mystic and me, we are masterpieces.

Tracey Lipp

MICHELLE PALMER MCKENZIE: Michelle McKenzie is an SEO content writer and graphic designer with a focus on illustration and branding. She works from her cabin in beautiful Alberta with her two cats and some plants. Michelle can be reached through her personal hobby page on Instagram - Lalaland Art.

Email: michellepalmer1111@yahoo.com

LOVE & HEALING

LALALAND – A SAFE PLACE TO BE

> *I had surrounded myself with people telling me who I am. My value as a human being intrinsically tied to their perception. With this as my focus, I had become invisible, no wonder I had felt so empty.*
>
> *– Michelle McKenzie*

One day a wise woman said, "this fucked up shit won't be my story" and she packed up and moved to Lalaland. That woman is me. There was no clear sign that read "turn left in 300m to Lalaland", no, it was much harder to find than just that and I happened upon it quite seemingly at the time, by accident.

You see, I had received the most heart-breaking news and I was feeling lonely, afraid, and vulnerable. This is not at all an unfamiliar set of emotions for me, as I have experienced them regularly throughout my life since learning and believing I was unlovable from a very young age. Prior to this point in my life I would have reacted to the news by say, drowning unlovable me in alcohol or seeking validation from others in one of various ways, but on this day instead, I picked up a set of markers and a fresh pad of paper.

I started drawing many painful memories for quite a while projecting all my old programs and experiences on to the page, desperate for my pain to be seen, known, acknowledged and understood by people I care about who had vanished from my life. Illustrating further, the clear evidence to justify how this had caused my own regrettable actions.

I wanted to be in a beautiful world full of flowers instead of the pool of regret in which I spent my days dwelling. My life at the time is best described in a poem by Emily Dickinson entitled *Remorse*.

> Remorse is memory awake,
> Her parties all astir,
> A presence of departed acts
> At window and at door
> It's past set down before the soul,
> And lighted with a match,
> Perusal to facilitate
> To help belief to stretch
> Remorse is cureless, the disease
> Not even God can heal,
> For tis his institution
> The complement of hell

I had lived in remorse hell at this point for almost two years. I realized how little others cared about how I felt and if that's the case then I must move on, besides, I was sick and tired of finding myself once again looking at my life through this hologram. Abandonment always brings me back to this very same view. I heard a saying that when you miss someone so much you lose yourself, that is love, I had to find myself.

I began by drawing simple flowers which turned into months of more flowers. Now, instead of sleeping the day away or zoning out to a television program I was falling asleep dreaming about concepts and waking up eager to create.

My initial pictures featured a girl in a long skirt with a pretty bow and ballet dancer slippers. She could be seen entering the doorways of various castles or hobbit homes. Originally, I strategically placed her that way because I felt I could not draw faces but over time I came to connect with the girl as myself looking for something, I believe she is looking everywhere to find a happy and safe universe in which to live, and I am

Lalaland – A Safe Place to Be

sure hoping she finds it! I became very curious about where my imagination wanted to take her next and about how to overcome my artistic limitations to achieve the desired effect of my image, this is something I want to continue to grow and expand by learning other mediums.

To this point I would visualize what I wanted to draw, and I would project it on the page and then impose the background. A fellow artist suggested I incorporate the background as part of the image – interesting how I myself was disconnected from my surroundings. I allowed the simple joy of creating to spill over into my own personal space, playing light jazz as I selected my colour schemes and taking breaks with a homemade London fog while sitting back to contemplate my progress and next steps. I found myself thinking - wow, what a beautiful day.

As I continued to draw, surreal flowers, zodiac stars and hippy vans brightly emerged on the page. I started to think about the use of colour and how it related to chakras and their meanings. I felt an inner peace I had never known and a deeper commitment to the journey.

I realized just how much the practice of creating took me away from focusing on my hologram. It brought me fully to the present moment and allowed me to turn inward with pure awareness of that which I really am. Finally, I had found where I want to live, right there at the tip of my marker and I call that place Lalaland.

I call it Lalaland because I had been told in the past that I lived there. Logically I knew this was true because I acknowledge that my trauma brain was projecting things differently than they were When I decided to dedicate more time to Lalaland, I thought initially it was another form of escape but to my great surprise it instead provided me the ability to see reality how it really is and not how my trauma brain projects it to be.

When I am creating, I feel a connection to source energy where loneliness does not exist. Art soothes my anger at injustice, when I feel "fight or flight" I can run anywhere by marker without repercussion to myself or others. I am no longer afraid as I am safe to express my feelings without the ridicule I received as a child and my emotions around that become regulated. In a world where vulnerability is seen as a weakness, art embraces it.

I started to breathe from my diaphragm, I took my Vitamin D and showered regularly. I began adhering to a sleep schedule and for the first time stopped obsessing about my bank account and future forecasting a certain life of destitution. The further I moved in to creating the farther away from fear I became. If I had markers, I was going to be okay. I learned to enjoy the process.

I haven't taken any Art Therapy courses and this is a goal of mine to learn more and to possibly teach Art Therapy one day. I imagine myself working with youth and doing art together so that they are not alone with their pain. My favourite drawings are where things lined up or turned out in the finished piece that were not at all planned by me "we don't make mistakes, just happy little accidents" as Bob Ross once said.

I am often surprised when I look back on my illustrations and see details that lend clues to my authentic self. I realized that up until this time I had surrounded myself with people telling me who I am. My value as a human being intrinsically tied to their perception. With this as my focus, I had become invisible, no wonder I had felt so empty. There is a saying that you can't see your face in boiling water. In the calm afternoon light dancing in amongst the doodles, how, dare I say, exciting it was to finally meet myself!

The most shocking realization was when I drew my latest picture "Bhujapid Asana – Shoulder Press" it is me, Lala, doing a yoga pose surrounded in bright yellow light. I simply drew it because I wanted to create something pretty. When I looked back on it later – two things happened. First, I looked up the meaning of yellow chakra - to be balanced in yellow chakra means energy, strength, confidence, strong will, mental balance, health, confidence, active. And there was Lala – balanced.

Secondly, it reminded me of a book (where the cover was completely yellow) that my grandmother had given to me on my third Birthday, she had written a personal message to me inside and the photo of her message is on my office wall. I decided I would look up the book itself online (as the original resides in a box in another province). I don't know how to word this in a way that it blows your mind like it did mine. The book is called "God is Everywhere – Discovering God's Love in the World" Illustrated by Mary Hamilton. On the very front cover pictured a girl

Lalaland – A Safe Place to Be

with a skirt, a bow and ballerina slippers. I then learned Mary Hamilton had gone on to create "Mary's Bears" for Hallmark and I had bought my daughter many of these figurines when she was small, proving that God is everywhere and involved in our lives whether we publicly acknowledge Him or not.

It is now half of a century later and I am opening this book. I am reminding myself that the best time to plant a tree was 30 years ago, and the second-best time is today.

I began posting my pictures online with the caption "Love, Health, Mental Health and Unity" because this is what I want for myself and for the world we live in. Nobody talks about how success may simply look like staying sober, going to bed early, not buying all the things and drawing. By doing my own inner work and healing I make suffering unfashionable, if you do it too, the human consciousness rises, one beautiful soul at a time.

It is my belief that human moral agency, not the deity or God, that are the cause of evil. Lalaland has a sign that says "keep out" as a reminder to recognize when my peace is disrupted and to disengage. I am learning discernment in the relationships that lift me up and those that drag me down. I have come to believe it is my obligation to be peaceful and to lower my environmental impact. I believe the more people that reconcile inwardly and become peaceful, the faster moral agency will dissolve.

One of my first pictures was inspired by the Rainforest Flying Squad at Fairy Creek. This group peacefully defends the last 3.5% of Old Growth Forest in British Columbia. I am inspired by all these people that live in alignment with their values and dedicate their lives to protecting this forest in the face of a punitive system hell bent on endless growth economies. I feel guilt around how many trees I printed advertising messages on in my past life due to my own greed. I feel the pull to create a painting of these warriors sitting with a tree called Big Lonely Doug. As I have just completed an entire season of Landscape Artist of the Year, I feel I'm ready to try acrylics! Perhaps if it works out better than my recent attempt at watercolour, I could deliver it as a gift this summer.

"An inability to visualize the future (let alone a positive future) is the hallmark of trauma" – Annie Wright. By way of the chapter that I wrote prior to this one, I leave my old hologram in the past. I want to thank someone who came into my life in the most unusual way, picture a shooting star. Her name is Gillian Stevens, and she is the author of a set of books entitled Explore, Transform, Flourish. It is through this connection that I was invited to write this chapter and through this exercise that I have grown exponentially.

With much gratitude I honour where I am, to be living in and surrounded by the beautiful nature and mountains on the traditional territory of Lheidli T'enneh in Northern BC. My art, my feelings and my words now connected, I open the book that was given to me at age three and I embark on my mission to discover God's Love in the world through the enjoyment and appreciation for the simple things in life – God is Everywhere.

Wishing you All - Love, Health, Mental Health, and Unity

Lalaland Art

Michelle McKenzie

SABRINA GISCÔMBE, MSW, RSW: Sabrina is a Registered Social Worker with a Master's degree in Social Work. She is also the co-founder of My Body Life Health Wellness, a wellness company that helps people with busy lifestyles learn how to nourish their bodies with foods that honor their health and their taste buds; stay active, and prioritize other self-care/personal care activities that tend to fall to the bottom of their 'to do' list -- especially during transitions like starting or growing a family, building a career, or business. Her business partner is her best friend and husband Michael Anthony Giscômbe, Certified Master Personal Trainer, Nutritionist & former US Marine. They wear other professional hats. Sabrina is a Service Manager at an organization that serves children, youth, and their families. She supervises a team of eight staff at the moment. Michael Anthony is also a Real Estate Agent. They have two children, ages eight and five.

> PRIORITIZING WELLNESS

THE DAY I BECAME A PRIORITY IN MY LIFE

> *We all can try to impact the lives of people around us in a good way by the little things we do.*
>
> *~ Sabrina Giscômbe*

Right now, at your fingertips, you have every self-care hack you can ever think of, inspired by health and wellness gurus around the world. My wellness page @myblhwellness on Instagram might be one of those feeds that inspire you. At this moment, billions of people all around the globe are accessing content on social media platforms that make them feel inspired to live their 'best life'. I am a sucker for aesthetically pleasing visuals that inspire the pursuit of slow-living and optimizing one's wellbeing. There was a time when I would follow accounts with content that made me feel like I had escaped my reality albeit temporarily from my busy stressful lifestyle. I still follow accounts that inspire me to be well but they no longer serve as a mechanism of escape from my reality. Habits are what have changed my reality and identity.

On June 28, 2021, I walked away from work habits that were no longer serving me and my family. I was finally becoming the type of person I had wanted to become. After fifteen years of working in a non-profit direct service setting where much of the work I did was crisis-oriented and urgent, I walked away. I remember vividly leaving an office that was deserted as it had been closed to the public and staff were working virtually and remotely in the community. I took the elevator from the seventh floor to the main level holding a large enough box full of items I had collected over the years and had kept at my desk – artwork from the children and youth I had helped, milestone gifts for the years of service at the agency, a set of cutlery, a couple of sentimental mugs, an almost empty box of herbal tea, a bottle of olive oil, soya sauce, stationery items, knickknacks, and photos of my family framed.

On the main level, there was no one in sight aside from a security guard to my left and a cashier at the Starbucks shop to my right. When I stepped outside of that high-rise building and walked towards my vehicle I felt the natural elements of the outdoors – the sunlight that made me squint and the increasing ground winds below. When you have been doing something for so long and it starts to become unhealthy for you, it can be difficult to take that first step towards doing something different that will benefit you.

These difficult moments mark the time when I became a priority in my life. I took a leap of faith and said yes to a leadership position in an organization where I knew no one that I would be working directly with. As a racialized Black female, born and raised in Toronto by a single parent I did what I had been taught which was to live by faith. I trusted that the boldness in which I had embodied was exactly what I needed to take my seat where God wanted me to be. How My Family Values Re-centered Me Over the years as a child protection worker I used my passion to encourage individual and family wellbeing by serving children, youth, and families and this became a purpose for me. However, my resilience as an essential worker was tested by the first wave of the coronavirus pandemic. Though I had a lower caseload of 16 families at the time, the families in which I served had complex trauma and their issues were compounded by the pandemic. I was also challenged personally by the lockdown and the impact it had on my household. My children, ages four and seven then were learning from home and I was working virtually and remotely in the community.

The Day I Became a Priority in My Life

Habits like working late and overextending myself due to a lack of boundaries crept in. As forgiving as my family was, these bad habits were compounding into negative dynamics in my household and marriage. My core value to have a strong family bond and marriage drove me to pivot and change my job.

I now work from home and support eight front-line workers that are doing the work I did for the past fifteen years. I am now able to put daily systems and processes in place for myself that set me and my family up for success.

My past work experiences and working within a supportive work culture have helped me to thrive right out of the gate as a supportive service manager. It is the positive side that has come from this pandemic. According to Donald McGannon, "Leadership is an action, not a position."

I am flourishing now not only in my health and relationships but as well in my new role within child welfare. Various factors have helped me to contribute to cultivating a healthier lifestyle for the employees I work with and support.

For one, I have reframed that their personal care and wellbeing is a public and solvable problem rather than a private matter that starts and ends with them. In a world where it seems like big changes are needed, I am reminded that we all can try to impact the lives of people around us in a good way by the little things we do. Saying hi and good morning on a virtual team chat each day for my team of eight is one way that I try to make up for the human touch moments that would normally happen organically in an office work environment. When my team meets virtually, we always start with a check-in and during that check-in, we state whether we can "give a coffee" or "need a coffee". This allows for people to feel freed up to be honest about how they are feeling without having to pour their hearts out on a screen. What I have observed is that organically staff that can give a coffee are reaching out to staff who said that they needed a coffee. These little acts of kindness can go a long way and we can all use it in the world right now. The late Desmond Tutu stated, "Do your little bit of good where you are; it's those little bits of good put together that overwhelm the world." Creating a team culture that I want to be a part of is paramount to me. If I noticed that a worker is working into the night or sending late emails I tell them to log off. I don't want them to overextend themselves. I also try to model the same. In addition to meeting staff every 6-weeks for supervision to discuss and check in with each staff to provide clinical direction on cases I not only see that they are doing their work, but also how they are feeling. I can encourage each employee to create and build healthier habits for themselves such as encouraging them to take breaks to do things that make their hearts happy. I get to know what sparks their joy and I am intentional in reminding them to follow through with habits that build resilience for themselves. For example, one staff finds joy in spotting cardinals when she goes for her morning walks with her dog. I make space for her to share these experiences in our one-on-one interactions as well as in team settings. Recently, I participated in a group consult for the Human Trafficking Committee that I am a member of at my agency. The staff who had requested the consult for expertise on how to work with a young person they suspected was at risk of being trafficked had mentioned that they had put in many hours working with the youth and their parent. That day the staff was scheduled to meet with the youth and their parent after work hours. I wondered about that staff and how he was doing, whether he had children, a family, and the impact that his work would have on him and his family. I circled back to the group in a subsequent group meeting about my observation and to my surprise, the staff's sibling was a committee member and had been triggered to check-in with her brother based on the observations I had made. After the meeting, the sibling of that staff sent me an email that confirmed for me at that moment that I was still encouraging individual and family wellbeing but this time by serving professionals that are working with clients. She expressed that she had reached out to her brother after the meeting to check-in with him as he does have small children and a family. She said that he appreciated the comments that she had shared I had made at the meeting. My inquiry sent a message to this employee that their wellness is important to us. The other committee members and I have included in our consults to practice checking in with staff how they are doing when

The Day I Became a Priority in My Life

they come to us for advice on cases. I was able to communicate to staff in the committee as well as my regular team of eight that there is a shift in the culture where prioritizing the wellbeing of employees in this work and working virtually is the focus. And that I am thrilled to be a part of the leadership where I too can impact and influence this change.

The situation of racialized Black staff and other equity-seeking groups working in predominantly racialized White communities brings about a need to provide anti-racist and trauma-informed support in supervision as these staff can be met with racism and discrimination when servicing clients. I have worked with staff who have experienced racism and discrimination on the job and have walked alongside them to find ways to ensure their safety as well as to address the behaviour as the agency does not tolerate hate that targets the identity of their employees.

The overwhelming response from staff that they appreciate that their wellbeing and health in the work and working virtually matters gives me a sense of job satisfaction. I want to give acknowledgment to the individuals and organizations that have supported me in gaining this understanding and reframing of wellness. It has helped me personally and has shaped me to be the leader and wellness professional I am today.

Sabrina Giscômbe, MSW, RSW

Jessica Flagiello: By day, Jessica Flagiello works as a sales and hospitality manager at various jobs; however, she imagines being a superhero at night in Toronto, Canada. She expertly crafts writings for operational strategies and innovative marketing plans for many companies to grow. She trains entrepreneurs in mind- setting techniques and also coaches soccer. When Jessica is not immersed working on leadership development presentations and outreach projects on a local and international level, you can find her meditating to feel grounded and happy. She practices a spiritual lifestyle with the Hare Krishna community where she has started several initiatives and serves on different programs. Her personal mantra is, "Keep moving forward." Her inspiration, encouragement, and appreciation has helped numerous people worldwide find their path that enriches and uplifts them. With her witty humour, authenticity, enthusiasm, and depth of wisdom that captures hearts and minds, she continues to improve with courage, passion, and a lot of laughter along the way. Jessica loves spending time with her family and friends, and getting into trouble with her nephews. She enjoys traveling the world with an itinerary, cooking, hiking in nature, star gazing, visiting museums, and playing sports. She is obsessed with collecting books, postcards from her trips, listening to music, and learning new things to master as she attempts to multitask. Jessica loves meeting new people and runs an international group called Connected Souls, which brings together positive like- minded compassionate individuals to feel enlivened. One of Jessica's dreams is to be a motivational speaker as she believes we can all make an impact by empowering the potential of others through connection and love. She co- authored a chapter entitled "Continue Courageously to be Empowered" in the book From Bottom To Top.

Facebook: Jessica Flagiello
Instagram: jessicaflag
Email: jessconnectedsouls@gmail.com.

> PRIORITIZING WELLNESS

FIGHTING FOR FORGIVENESS

> *"It's profound, all the hurt the heart can handle, and still hold on to hope."*
>
> *~ Jessica Flagiello*

Before you read this, please note that these words have been diluted in odium for years and are only fragments of my private expressions. I lived in obscurity because darkness was all I knew. Nevertheless, lately I have created and abide a meaningful serene life. I changed my inner aspects to improve and motivate me forward. Inevitable, my harmony was under examination to see if I truly altered. In mid-August, there was a fight and a violent act had been committed upon me. I wish I could explain the episode, but my thoughts stumble on the page because my hand was unable to keep up. As I scrambled to put words together they became out of sync; as it is a perfect reflection of my mind. I desire to articulate myself in length, fluidity, and depth; still I won't admit how draining it is. I become fixated to craft flawless lines; trying to depict my emotions so other understand. I imagined living through my sorrows heroically, but this story of destruction and growth is filled with my intentions, self-discovery, and personal transformation; similar what happens to a caterpillar's journey in the cocoon state to a butterfly. I know everything happens for a reason and life tests the limits of our soul just to build character.

    I walked alone on the path; the sun shined brightly and clouds drifted apart. Shouts intoxicated the woods as a man ran towards me. I inhaled deeply and prepared for the push. I felt hands on my shoulders as my feet stepped irregularly to ensure I wouldn't fall; yet, my balance failed. I was knocked to the ground; my body slammed incongruously, twisting to move as it adjusted from the deformed position that I landed in. My own arm wrapped around my neck; with the other hand griping the soil, trying to lift myself up. I wondered, "Am I going to die?" Due to the lack of oxygen, I laid motionless and my brain struggled to stay alive, while my body was willing something else. I disregard all the unvalued wishes I made before and only begged for air and help; but he didn't conform to my request to release me. This assault was caused by a disagreement and I didn't plan to hurt him. I felt like a caterpillar; crawling on the earth, unnoticed and grotesque. I was fighting for life; scraping by and latching on like other insects always under scrutiny and attack. My body was trembling from the beating but my mind reinsured me that it would stop. I needed help. I was exhausted from what I had endured but my heart was enthusiastic by love and forgiveness already. As I was covered by dirt; I envied those creatures that were not controlled by another and thought how precious, uncertain, and lack of time we have. I eliminated anger from my being or else it would have broken me and I would have been a memory. Something astonishing happened as I looked up and saw in the distance a blue figure swaying between trees; almost cleverly keeping my attention on him so I wouldn't lose hope. Another older man appeared standing, observing and contemplating to intervene. He too, captivated my conscious and all my energy focused on breathing. Even as my sight diminished, their outlines kept their depth of details. I felt peaceful by their presence as I assumed this was an evaluation; that impelled and guided me forward. I aspired in those moments that my inspirational survival story might help others overcome their challenges; so I vowed to live. I realized my intentions were authentic and didn't want to fight as it wasn't my nature. I was confident in knowing there

Fighting for Forgiveness

were people looking over me. I finally got free; as I arose and the trees, rocks, soil and animals claimed their spots on the ground again. A loving force led me in controlling my despondency. I remained silent as I dragged myself towards a place of acceptance and refuge. Nevertheless, I didn't find sanctuary there and it failed me. I was feeling exasperation of the annoyance of corruption to one's soul and moved on with caution. My inner vulnerabilities were exposed and I was unwilling to live in an abyss as I did everything to rise above the shadows. The melancholy part was everyone abandoned me. It was overwhelming and pathetic no one protected me. Sadly, mental destruction overpowered me as my brain was racing, tripping and rolling down upon its own thoughts, trying to get away from it-self. I was a master of masking my mistakes but an expert in examining others emotions. My disgusting bodily caterpillar scurried away and left a repulsive trail that no one followed. I retreated and wandered to escape myself; how pitiful to lose oneself in oneself. I walked for hours and finally sat by the lake looking at the vast openness and perceived my life as insignificant. I was feeling alone and annihilated because my heartbroken words were out of reach but never been so loud before. I demanded silence, except the noise kept me company and soon it departed. I experienced an irrepressible bondage to loneliness and the separation amplified my longing; thus, I relinquished and cried freely. I deliberated who those men were and prayed for strength. It was vital to believe this was a trial and necessary to acquire peace and wisdom. Even feeling lost, my hope was finding an opportunity of growth in destruction; just as the caterpillar travels onwards in their journey; I too had to be compassionate in my aim of progress. Despite pain being unbearable, I had to fight for forgiveness with them.

Weeks later, I had insomnia because I reflected about my insecurities; questioning my perception of all my old impurities which were my only recollections of the event. By protecting my sanity, my heart couldn't rest as nightmares arrived. Anxiety crept in, causing depression and I feared an eclipse in my life would occur again. The emptiness echoed as it was ephemeral and my memoires tormented me. I could run on empty but it is the emptiness that people feel and I never anticipated damaging myself or others. My mind kept busy; thinking its invincible but only learning its entangled by the desire to feel understood, needed and wanted. I never imagined myself hubris, but believing that, was a sign of my immaturity protruding. Humility was the remedy to rid the nuisances of desperation. I tortured and neglected myself; being utterly alone and catastrophic by enmity. I became bewildered in isolation anguish; losing myself in the illness of destruction, fear and confinement. The caterpillar encloses itself, making a protective cocoon in order to undergo metamorphosis. I also had to enter a new stage as a pupa so I could adjust my structure and modify. During this growth of evolution, I became fearless in emerging out of the intense pressure and couldn't forfeit on becoming conscious and appreciative. It's profound, all the hurt the heart can handle, and still hold on to hope. At that moment; I started the process of discovering features of my soul as I always had a spirituality inclination. I embraced my solitude and the notion of forgiveness started, filled and ended my view. As I stared at my challenges; I prayed and knew immediately they would be chances to be reinvigorated with passion, patience, and empathy. I was determined to be self-aware and find purpose but I first had to find connections with myself and admiration for God. I eagerly practiced a pious life; engaging fully as I knew all apprehensiveness I accumulated would vanish or dissolve like the outer layer of a cocoon shell. Love occupied my being and slowly I trusted the process and became happy. Similar to a caterpillar that sheltered itself to produce its wings; I absorbed my attention in learning as my need for growth outweighed the suffering. Although the evolution was treacherous; I had to fight for forgiveness with myself.

    I couldn't allow myself to be consumed by the revulsion of the incident that had built up in my life anymore. I concluded, to move on I had to orchestrate my heart, body, spirit and mind until they achieved the accurate affirmation. It was ambitious but acquitting empowered me to find compassion and understanding for others. Mental annihilation and forgiveness were the only pure agony and cure. Faith assisted me to improve by transforming doubts that use to captivate me in misery into optimistic beliefs. The influential spiritual wisdom that I gathered united, healed, and uplifted me. As I broke through layers that sealed me in; I appeared magnificent and prepared for my journey of reaching my

Fighting for Forgiveness

potential. 'Courage: the weak can never forgive; forgiveness is the attribute of the strong.' (Gandhi) I accepted everything happens for a reason and my inflicted distress gave me numerous opportunities to grow. I felt liberated; just as the butterfly emerges, cleans itself off, flaps its wings and ascends to the sky. I desired freedom to fly and share essential love as I never wanted anyone to experience that pain. The cultivation of humility by practicing gratitude, nourished my innate ability to transcend life's circumstances and eliminate the frustration of feeling incomplete. This spiritual renewal raised my conscious and I became calm in tribulations. I understood the soul is eternally, blissful and full of knowledge and by serving others we experience deep affection that exceeds our expectations. I believe we all want to be happy, maintain our happiness and above all- give happiness to others as we navigate to find our own meaning in life. Associating with spiritual individuals, I continued my efforts in making progress of improving myself and feeling inner fulfillment. My old constant perplex lamentations gave me reasons to explore my soul; allowing me to share transcendental knowledge with others so they would find the courage, tolerance, and sincerity to keep moving forward. I transformed my bitter past into a better future and am still working on becoming the best version of myself as I didn't want to weep in weakness any longer. Like a butterfly that thought its journey ended when everything seemed disconsolate, was actually its tremendous triumph. In recognizing my own potential; I obtained unflinching devotion as my prosperous qualities were presented when I am equanimity. As I reassessed the affair, I concluded that the two individuals in the woods that disastrous day were spiritual beings protecting me. Their manifestation revealed that I am never alone and my existence is worth everything. Realizing this, I acknowledged all turmoil situations are part of my story and a chance to transform into my most excellent self. Forgiveness was the root of my adjustment to accelerate and amplify upwards like a butterfly. Meditating granted me the capacity to proceed peacefully towards my altitude and emulate glorious people characteristics. My aptitude shined and I soared as I rebuilt myself and wanted to make an impact on the world. I converted my energy in revolutionizing my condition of life and increasing my mindfulness and steadiness. Though my alteration was noticeable, I had to fight for forgiveness with everyone to make them understand my changes.

As I finished writing this narrative, I felt equipoised as the burden of carrying this memory fell away and disappeared while I prepared to lose things that held me down. The fight enraged me but I was more disappointed that it aggravated my tranquility as it was under observation and I had to learned how to deal with it. Resources enabled me to consistently look within for realization, illuminate outward to support, rise above every occasion, and go beyond any obstacle that comes my way. My life consisted of ameliorating and managing my emotions so I would improve all aspects and keep moving forward on my journey. This motivated me to be my best and make progress in overcoming challenges with humility. As others saw me constantly jubilant and harmonious; however, this was not always the case since only few really knew what I have gone through to achieve these accomplishments and be who I am today. I was ashamed and I encapsulated this account until it was euphony and the pain subsided. Advancements in spirituality is assessed by the profoundness of one's genuine compassion, forgiveness and development of being selfless. Comprehending these values I began fully utilizing this chance to attain a purified, pleasurable, and ultimate living state. I found deep connection with myself and God as I searched my soul to identify how I can serve others. I remembered a monk said, "How does one become a butterfly? - One must desire to fly so much that they give up being a caterpillar." Believing this statement; my nature materialized and provided me with relief from my suffering and the concept of a better life. I did not want to die alone in the woods; so I promised, if I lived I would be brave and graceful just as those outline people did as they gave me hope in the greatest despair. As the caterpillar wriggles along the earth trying to detect its way at the start of their life; I sensed the same as I strolled without directions and was engrossed with calamities but my objective never wavered. The pupa entraps and recluse itself; just as I imprisoned and encircled myself in solitary to find answers to dilemmas. As an exquisite butterfly surfaces through the cocoon; I also immersed myself in the sun and freedom as I couldn't fail myself and had to reach my potential of being truly happy. My faith inspired,

Fighting for Forgiveness

encouraged and appreciated my movement forward. By learning and sharing wisdom, it allowed me to accept, understand, need and want my own self as I aspired to develop my passions. My growth from destruction enlightened me to live with authentic intentions, discover my real self, and transform my inner personality to find noble meaning in life. My consciousness considered my soul being tested by a higher power and knew the reason why everything happens is to give me the opportunity to improve and help others find their way. This experiences aided me to become my own butterfly and promoted me to fly on my own as I advocate everything can empower someone as long as we fight, grow and move on from it, the possibilities are endless. This story of survival is just a chapter of my life but has given me my life to fight for. I found forgiveness for fighting but I fought for freedom to forget.

OLIVIA WHITEMAN: Olivia is a two-time best-selling author. She is amazed by this as a car accident left her with short term memory, an inability to stay focused, and fatigue. Despite setbacks, she is a talented speaker and gives talks to entrepreneurs on her three-pillar system to get accountability, greater awareness of what has them stuck and how to move forward so they can achieve greater financial success in their business. In addition, her legacy planning course and workbook is praised by estate attorneys. It helps people prepare everything for when they pass so their family can remember and celebrate them. Her book includes checklists and journal prompts that a family will find valuable and future generations will treasure. Olivia loves honoring family and feels strongly that people should leave a legacy behind through sharing their stories. In June of 2022, she completed *Honoring Dad Every Day*, a compilation book available on Amazon that she created that gives tributes, quotes, and journal prompts dedicated to fathers. She lives in the United States yet loves connecting through Zoom with people from all over the world.

PRIORITIZING WELLNESS

LEAVE A LEGACY FOR YOUR FAMILY

> *My dear friend died with no will... I guess she thought she would do it tomorrow. Tomorrow never came for her. I thought, I did not want that to happen to other people. I started to wonder what information we need to have ready should something happen to us...*
>
> *- Olivia Whiteman*

Have you ever wanted to know more about your family who are no longer around?

I have. Of course, I could talk to older relatives, look through old, faded photos, hoping there is a date, or a name written on the back that will lead me to more clues.

I could also spend hours digging up information going through old birth certificates, passports, and historical documents hoping to find additional hints to help me learn more. I mean what can you tell by a signature or a date on a document? If there is no additional information that goes with it, all I can do is make guesses. Wouldn't it be nice if there was more available, firsthand? I think so. So, I decided to do something about it.

I created a workbook, and a course where you can document your stories along with your assets allowing future generations in your family tree to not feel as I do, wanting more.

Hearttalks

I was inspired to do this during the start of the COVID pandemic, a friend who I talked to daily, got infected. She died shortly afterwards. She was a wellness and health professional and never gave any thought to not being around for a long time. The fact that her family members lived well into their nineties, made her think it would be the same for her. My dear friend died with no will, no life insurance, no documents sharing her wishes. She left a mess. I guess she thought she would do it tomorrow.

Tomorrow never came for her. I thought, I did not want that to happen to other people. I started to wonder what information we need to have ready should something happen to us when we are no longer around to share our thoughts and wishes. Things like who to contact, funeral arrangements, and ways to avoid unnecessary expenses came to mind.

As reading became a problem for me, after a car accident, I researched videos to find everything I could on the topic. I even discovered items I did not consider thinking about. When it came to looking things up, I was very thorough. It's more like I was very insecure. The lesson I learned from this experience is that even though you may not have confidence in yourself, it doesn't mean it is true.

After the car accident left me with cognitive issues-- short term memory, problems focusing, severe headaches, fatigue, inability to think straight and unable to write. I was very insecure which had me convinced that I could not write a book.

I did not let my disempowering thoughts stop me. I had to find a way. I was on a mission to prevent other people from dying and leaving their family unprepared to handle things. I got a word processing software, a grammar checking program and a top-rated microphone that transcribes your voice into text. The microphone was the key element. I could only work a very short time each day before I was exhausted, yet I persevered.

I had friends read the book back to me, as it was very hard for me to focus on written words. When the book was completed which took a very long time to do, I asked and got proof reading and editing help from my best-friend Joan. It is great to have friends; they make life sweeter.

Leave A Legacy For Your Family

When another friend showed my workbook to the attorney working on her family's estate, he responded, "This is really good," and topped off the compliment by buying 100 copies for his clients. It felt amazing.

What I did not expect after finishing the book was how much more confident about myself, I would start to feel. I wrote other books and one of the books that I put together with other authors, *Harmony in Chakras Volume II, - Emotions* made it to best seller status. It shifted something inside of me.

The one thing the lawyer was not interested in was the section that lets you share your stories and family photos. I didn't initially plan on adding a place to add stories. It was after I gathered the information that I thought about my own family tree and realized, it's not enough to just lists contact information, passcodes, assets, financials, and heirlooms. People need to leave behind their stories, their legacy.

I thought, if I made it simple for them by asking questions like, what did you think about your mom? Did you have good relationships? Where did she grow up? How did your mommy and daddy meet? It would be easier for people to write things down.

I remember one time, I was sitting near a man and a woman talking and could overhear their conversation. He asked her, "Where did your mother grow up?" She answered, "I don't know." He said, "What do you mean you do not know." She replied, "We never talked about it." He came back with, "What do you mean you never talked about it?" She responded, "It must have been something she couldn't talk about." She then started questioning him. "How did your parent's meet? He responded, "I don't know." She replied, "Well I know how my parents met. I know exactly how and where they met, how they feel in love and how long they dated before they got married." He just replied, "Touché."

I guess the thing that I am trying to say is we do not always know all the information about our families, but whatever we know is valuable. What I also learned is not to push people to give you information they are not ready to give because we do not know what traumas people have been through. Maybe they will never talk about it, but just maybe they are writing things down and plan to gift you the answers you are seeking when they are no longer around.

Hearttalks

My hope is that you agree that stories about your life are helpful to add a deeper understanding of who you are. If you think about it people have been through a lot-- wars, abuse, difficult situation that they had no control over, and perhaps do not want to think about. They also have stories about winning spelling bees, being the top of their class, buying their dream house or how they became the president of a major company.

You never know where life takes you. Just know that recording your experiences allows, one day your progeny to know you better, and when your family reads your stories, they will accept your words and feel as much gratitude, as they would in finding treasure.

When I was sharing what I was working on with people, some shared that they had no children. I could not help thinking that may be true, yet your sister has children, and one day their children will have children.

In addition, your aunt's and your aunt's kids will, and one day they can read what you went through, what you triumphed and struggled with. This information can give them something special that you cannot even imagine today. Like in my case, maybe one day, my great-nephews or nieces will ask their parents about their family's roots, and they would learn in their family there was this woman who lost confidence in herself after an accident left her feeling lost and confused most of the day, yet she accomplished so much. Maybe one of them will think, "I don't believe in myself. Maybe I can be like her and maybe I, too, can accomplish a lot." I think that would be awesome.

I, therefore, encourage and remind people that writing down their stories is not necessarily for their benefit, but for their family who will someday be looking for them. I trust and hope you agree with me.

What I also experienced is that good feelings last only so long. I soon began to realize that a lot of people who got the workbook were not filling it out. They got overwhelmed by its size. I didn't know what to do until someone shared, "Why don't you break it up into a lot of different books?" That is exactly what I did. One category, I thought of was finances and assets. I thought about the person who thinks that this is the most important thing they need to record. Although I agree that providing this information is very valuable. I want to encourage such

Leave A Legacy For Your Family

an individual to also let their family understand their relationship with money more. I, therefore, added prompts like, "what did it feel like to make money for the first time" or 'how much did you earn on your first job."

I remember a friend of mine once said that he was so happy he worked, worked, worked, and gave his father all the money to hold for him. One day, he asked his dad for his money and his father shared that he took all his money to buy something that was needed for the house. My friend shared how horrible he felt. He told me, "That was my money to do with what I wanted. I worked for it." He shared how that incident affected his life. Even though he turned out to be an over-achiever financially, he always feels that someone will take his money away from him.

I believe including these kinds of stories can help because I believe we not only inherit DNA for our hair color and eye color, but we also inherit other things, spiritual things from our ancestors as well, and we do not know where these gifts or traumas came from. I strongly encourage people to include these kinds of things and have therefore added related journal prompts to all eight of my workbook categories.

People want to know that even though you can't spell anymore, you can still write a book. It doesn't stop you. Only you can stop you, and so in this heart-to-heart talk, all I want to share is a wish for you to plant a legacy for your family.

If you feel like you do not have a nuclear family, just remember we are all connected, and even though you may think you are not thought about, people are thought about.

It is no surprise that when someone passes away, who do they call? The family (this includes the people they hold dear to their heart and consider them as part of their family). When there is a wedding, who do they call? The family. People do not see each other for three years, suddenly, there is a wedding, and everybody who can attends. They take trains, planes, Ubers, and everybody comes out because they want to be part of family. So, record those legacy stories. Think of all the lost history we have because people did not write down stories about themselves.

For those of you, depending on your ethnicity or circumstances, who realize not everybody can trace their heritage or can find out about their ancestors beyond a generation or two, this is even more reason why you should write things down and start to make it easy for your family to trace their family line.

Let people know about your heirlooms, your assets, and your stories. And if you have no monetary assets, you have other assets. You have your life. That is the biggest asset, and you should love yourself for exactly who you are. By the way, I want to encourage you to discover your ancestors so much, as well as to be prepared when a family member dies, that I want to give you two gifts: Five Top Tools to Help You Track Down Your Ancestors and 10 Ways to Save Money When a Family Member Passes Away, both are FREE and given with my heart. Visit OliviaWhiteman.com/bonuses.

In conclusion, I am Olivia, and I would hope that you would love to invest in your family's legacy by completing one of my workbooks or courses. I end with a wish for you to have a beautiful life and to know that you are worth whatever it is that you want to do.

Olivia Whiteman

www.ingramcontent.com/pod-product-compliance
Lightning Source LLC
Chambersburg PA
CBHW070427010526
44118CB00014B/1937